AF754603

Dynamic Models and Their Applications in Emerging Markets

Centre for the Study of Emerging Markets Series

Series Editor: **Dr. Sima Motamen-Samadian**

The Centre for the Study of Emerging Markets (CSEM) Series will provide a forum for assessing various aspects of emerging markets. The series will include the latest theoretical and empirical studies from both academics and practitioners in relation to the economies and financial markets of emerging markets. These will cover a wide range of subjects, including stock markets and their efficiency in emerging markets, forecasting models and their level of accuracy in emerging markets, dynamic models and their application in emerging markets, sovereign debt and its implications, exchange rate regimes and their merits, risk management in emerging markets, derivative markets and hedging decisions in emerging markets, and governance and risk in emerging markets.

The series will be one of the main sources of reference on emerging markets, both within and outside those markets, for academics, national and international agencies, and financial institutions.

Titles include:

Sima Motamen-Samadian (*editor*)
DYNAMIC MODELS AND THEIR APPLICATIONS IN EMERGING MARKETS

Other Books by the Editor:

INTERNATIONAL DEBT AND CENTRAL BANKING IN THE 1980s (*with Z. Res*)

EMERGING MARKETS: Past and Present Experiences, and Future Prospects (*with C. Garido*)

Centre for the Study of Emerging Markets Series
Series Standing Order ISBN 1–4039–9521–4

You can receive future titles in this series as they are published by placing a standing order. Please contact your bookseller or, in case of difficulty, write to us at the address below with your name and address, the title of the series and one of the ISBNs quoted above.

Customer Services Department, Macmillan Distribution Ltd, Houndmills, Basingstoke, Hampshire RG21 6XS, England

Dynamic Models and Their Applications in Emerging Markets

Edited by

Sima Motamen-Samadian

palgrave macmillan

Selection and editorial matter © Sima Motamen-Samadian 2005
Individual chapters © Contributors 2005

All rights reserved. No reproduction, copy or transmission of this publication may be made without written permission.

No paragraph of this publication may be reproduced, copied or transmitted save with written permission or in accordance with the provisions of the Copyright, Designs and Patents Act 1988, or under the terms of any licence permitting limited copying issued by the Copyright Licensing Agency, 90 Tottenham Court Road, London W1T 4LP.

Any person who does any unauthorized act in relation to this publication may be liable to criminal prosecution and civil claims for damages.

The authors have asserted their rights to be identified as the authors of this work in accordance with the Copyright, Designs and Patents Act 1988.

First published in 2005 by
PALGRAVE MACMILLAN
Houndmills, Basingstoke, Hampshire RG21 6XS and
175 Fifth Avenue, New York, N.Y. 10010
Companies and representatives throughout the world.

PALGRAVE MACMILLAN is the global academic imprint of the Palgrave Macmillan division of St. Martin's Press, LLC and of Palgrave Macmillan Ltd. Macmillan® is a registered trademark in the United States, United Kingdom and other countries. Palgrave is a registered trademark in the European Union and other countries.

ISBN-13: 978–1–4039–9152–2 hardback
ISBN-10: 1–4039–9152–9 hardback

This book is printed on paper suitable for recycling and made from fully managed and sustained forest sources.

A catalogue record for this book is available from the British Library.

Library of Congress Cataloging-in-Publication Data

Dynamic models and their applications in emerging markets / edited by Sima Motamen-Samadian.
p. cm.—(Centre for the Study of Emerging Markets series)
Includes bibliographical references.
ISBN 1–4039–9152–9
1. Finance – Developing countries – Econometric models.
2. Credit – Developing countries – Econometric models.
3. Investments – Developing countries – Econometric models.
4. Risk management – Developing countries. I. Motamen-Samadian, Sima.
II. Series.

HG195.D96 2005
331′.01′5195—dc22 2004065451

10 9 8 7 6 5 4 3 2 1
14 13 12 11 10 09 08 07 06 05

Printed and bound in Great Britain by
Antony Rowe Ltd, Chippenham and Eastbourne

Contents

List of Figures

List of Tables

Preface

The six studies that are presented in this volume have been put together to provide a new insight into the application of dynamic models to emerging markets. The objective is to identify the most appropriate models to explain the behaviour of financial and macroeconomic variables in emerging economies – models that can be used by both practitioners and policymakers in pricing securities and dealing with macroeconomic variables. In this respect, after the introductory chapter, Chapter 2 examines the behaviour of interest rates in the Czech Republic. Chapter 3 highlights the role of regulatory and institutional factors in the default and credit risk of banks and reports on the findings in 34 emerging economies in Asia, Latin America and Central and Eastern Europe. Chapter 4 presents a dynamic analysis of default risk in the sovereign bond markets of four Latin American countries. Here the author applies a long memory model to the sovereign bond markets of Argentina, Brazil, Mexico and Venezuela and measures the extent of default risk contagion between these markets. Chapter 5 presents an empirical analysis of the behaviour of short- and long-term Euro interest rates and determines the most appropriate model specification for pricing Eurobonds. Inflation targeting is the subject of Chapter 6, where the author compares the effectiveness of the anti-inflationary monetary policies of 12 emerging economies in Latin America, Asia and Africa and reports on the benefits of an inflation-targeting policy. Chapter 7 provides a neo-Keynesian dynamic analysis of external debt and growth in emerging economies.

The volume will be of interest to all those who are working on dynamic models and wish to gain a better understanding of the behaviour of financial markets in emerging economies.

Acknowledgements

This volume is a collection of some of the papers that were presented at the International Conference on Emerging Markets and Global Risk Management in June 2004 in London. The conference was organized by the Centre for the Study of Emerging Markets (CSEM) at Westminster Business School. In this respect my sincere thanks go to Hanna Scobie at the European Economic and Financial Centre and to Len Shackleton at Westminster Business School, who inspired and supported me in organizing the conference.

My special thanks go to Ben Nowman, who graciously provided his help and support whenever I needed him, and to Frances Eckulugu, who generously helped me throughout the period when I was organizing the conference. I am also indebted to Shobhana Madhavan for all her valuable advice and to Mike Hodd for his continuous encouragement. I would also like to thank Stephen Rutt and Jacky Kippenberger for providing me with the opportunity to produce this volume and the CSEM Series.

Last but not least I would like to thank my family and in particular my husband, Vahab Samadian, for backing me all the way.

Notes on the Contributors

Christophe J. Godlewski is a Research Fellow and Lecturer in Management and Finance at the Laboratoire de Recherche en Gestion et Economie (LaRGE), Université Robert Schuman (Strasbourg III), France.

Edgardo Jovero is a Researcher at the Universidad Complutense de Madrid, Spain.

Alfonso Mendoza V. is a Professor of Economics and Finance at the Escuela de Economía, Universidad de Guanajuato, Mexico, and a part-time lecturer at the University of Liverpool, UK.

Sima Motamen-Samadian is the Director of the Centre for the Study of Emerging Markets and a Principal Lecturer in Economics at Westminster Business School, University of Westminster, UK.

Rebeca I. Muñoz Torres is a Researcher at the Department of Economics, University of Leicester, UK.

Khalid B. Nowman is the Director of Finance and Financial Services Research Cluster and a Principal Lecturer at Westminster Business School, University of Westminster, UK.

Kadom J. A. Shubber is a Senior Lecturer in Finance at Westminster Business School, University of Westminster, UK.

Harry Thapar is a Senior Lecturer in Finance at Westminster Business School, University of Westminster, UK.

1 Introduction

Sima Motamen-Samadian

One of the important factors that can affect the decision of investors to move to an emerging economy is the degree of economic and financial stability of that country. Financial communities are keen to know the extent to which movements in the macroeconomic variables of a country can be reliably predicted. The efficiency of forecasts and the effectiveness of policies depend on the correct specification of the models that are used in explaining the behaviour of variables. Given the large number of parameters and factors that can affect the behaviour of macroeconomic and financial variables over time, it is crucially important to use appropriate dynamic models that can better explain the performance of variables. The studies included in this volume have all tried to determine the most suitable model to explain the behaviour of financial markets in various emerging economies.

In Chapter 2, Ben Nowman and Kadom Shubber use a number of continuous time models of interest rates to determine the behaviour of short-term interest rates in the Czech Republic. By applying these models, which differ in terms of the relationship between the level and volatility of interest rates, the authors try to capture various aspects of interest rates, including drift and mean reversion. Their empirical results reveal the correct specification of this relationship, which is crucial for determining the most suitable model to compute implied bond prices for the Czech Republic. Nowman and Shubber show that for the Czech Republic, the parameter that measures the relationship between the level and volatility effect of interest rates is much higher than that assumed by most other theoretical models.

Excess credit risk and banks' default risk in emerging markets has been the subject of numerous studies. It is very important to understand the relationship between the regulatory, legal and institutional environment and banks' health. Yet few studies have actually dealt with the impact of these factors on banks' risk-taking and their probability of default. Christophe Godlewski, in Chapter 3, examines the application of default prediction models to banks in emerging economies. Here the author investigates the impact of regulatory and institutional factors on banks' risk-taking behaviour. He applies a two-step logit model to a sample of banks in 34 emerging economies and shows that the institutional and regulatory environment can become a source of excess credit risk and increase banks' risk of failure.

Credit risks are also analysed by Alfonso Mendoza in Chapter 4, where he examines the features of four Latin American sovereign bond markets, namely, those of Argentina, Brazil, Mexico and Venezuela. Mendoza proposes a family of credit risk models to capture three salient features of these markets: individual long-range dependency in volatility (or long memory, LM), high fractional comovement and time-varying risk premia. He then tries to measure the extent of default risk contagion in these markets during the 1990s and discovers evidence of LM. His results also suggest that the responses of bond spread changes to volatility shocks are not statistically different across countries, thus indicating that a common source may be driving all these markets. He also finds that the extent of fractional comovement is high and that the magnitude of the risk premia for investing in these bond markets is substantial. In this respect the family of bivariate fractional integrated GARCH-in-mean models that Mendoza offers appears to perform statistically better than the models of Brunetti and Christopher (2000) and Teyssière (1998). Finally Mendoza shows that policies aimed at limiting sudden contagion shocks may be of limited use and costly, and that hedging in these markets may become unreliable and lead to heavy losses.

The behaviour of short- and long-term Euro interest rates is an important factor that can affect the pricing of Eurobonds. Determination of this behaviour is discussed in Chapter 5. Here Ben Nowman and Harry Thapar use the Gaussian estimation methods of Nowman (1977, 2001) to estimate a two-factor continuous time model of Euro interest rates. They estimate three models of interest rates to capture various aspects of interest rate behaviour, including drift and mean reversion. The three models used are those of (1) Chan, Karolyi, Longstaff and Sanders (CKLS), (2) Vasicek and (3) Cox, Ingersoll and Ross (CIR). These models differ in the way they explain the relationship between the level and volatility of interest rates and the way they are allowed to be correlated in their two-factor form. Their empirical results show that there is a strong relationship between the volatility and the level of one-month Euro interest rates compared with the 1-year Euro rates. This is an important result that has serious implications for pricing Euro-denominated bonds.

Inflation targeting (IT) is becoming a very popular monetary rule in many countries. Rebeca I. Muñoz Torres, in Chapter 6, examines the effectiveness of IT policies using 11 emerging economies as case studies: 6 with IT and 5 without. These countries are Brazil, Chile, Israel, Mexico, Nigeria, the Philippines, South Africa, South Korea, Turkey, Uruguay and Venezuela. She divides the countries into two groups according to whether they adopted IT, and measures the sacrifice ratio (the output cost of disinflation) for each group. In assessing the impact of IT on these economies she follows three steps. First she identifies the disinflationary episodes for individual countries, then she estimates their aggregate supply curves and finally she employs a structural vector autoregressive (VAR) model. Her results clearly reveal that in countries where the process of disinflation has been accompanied by the implementation of explicit inflation targets, sacrifice ratios have either declined over time or else increased less than in other countries. Accordingly she concludes that countries that adopted inflation targeting have achieved both lower and more stable levels of inflation.

External debt and growth in emerging markets is the subject of the last chapter, where Edgardo Jovero provides a dynamic analysis from a neo-Keynesian perspective. Here the author develops an open-economy neo-Keynesian model in which market powers can be a source of indeterminacy and structural instability. Jovero argues that different countries with the same fundamentals might have varying experiences of growth and external debt. Structural instability in these countries can take the form of a Hopf bifurcation, with an increasing likelihood as the markup power increases. Using the qualitative geometric theory of nonlinear complex dynamic systems, Jovero presents evidence of how Hopf bifurcation might occur. Accordingly he rejects the neoclassical view of uniqueness and stability in the aggregate economy, in which agents are endowed with rational expectations and perfect foresight. Instead, he puts forward a Keynesian view that global structural instability can exist in the aggregate economy. He then goes on to present a policy of dampened fluctuations as an alternative to alleviate this instability.

References

Brunetti, C. and Christopher, L. (2000), Bivariate FIGARCH and fractional cointegration, *Journal of Empirical Finance* 7, 509–30.

Nowman, K. B. (1997), Gaussian estimation of single-factor continuous time models of the term structure of interest rates, *Journal of Finance* 52, 1695–706.

Nowman, K. B. (2001), Gaussian estimation and forecasting of multi-factor term structure models with an application to Japan and the United Kingdom, *Asia Pacific Financial Markets* 8, 23–34.

Teyssière, G. (1998), Multivariate long-memory ARCH modeling for high frequency foreign exchange rates, *GREQAM* 98.

2

Continuous Time Dynamic Modelling of Interest Rates in Emerging Markets

Khalid B. Nowman and Kadom J. A. Shubber

2.1 Introduction

The modelling of short-term interest rates in emerging markets is an important research area, especially in view of the growth of new financial markets and of the financial securities traded in these countries. Over the last decade, a number of researchers have looked at different models of short-term interest rates. An important paper in this area is the study by Chan, Karolyi, Longstaff and Sanders (1992, CKLS hereafter), who considered various one-factor models nested in their general interest rate model. The CKLS general model captured various aspects of interest rate behaviour, including drift and mean reversion of interest rates. It also allowed for a general relationship between the level of interest rates and the volatility of rates. By imposing restrictions on these parameters, various well-known models in the literature that are used extensively by financial market operators can be utilized.

These include the models of Merton (1973); Vasicek (1977); Cox, Ingersoll and Ross (1985, CIRSR thereafter); Dothan (1978); Brennan and Schwartz (1980, BR–SC hereafter); Cox, Ingersoll and Ross (1980, CIRVR hereafter); Cox (1975; Cox and Ross, 1976; the constant elasticity of variance, CEV, model) and the Geometric Brownian motion (GBM) model. Using the generalized methods of moments estimation method and an approximate discrete time model, CKLS found that for the US market there was a strong relationship of magnitude 1.5 between the volatility of rates and the level of rates. They also found weak evidence of mean reversion in interest rates.

These models have been tested extensively in various international markets; for example, Dahlquist (1996) considered Denmark, Sweden, Germany and the UK, Hiraki and Takezawa (1997) considered Japan and Tse (1995) looked at 11 different countries. One of the general conclusions reached in these studies is that there are differences in the link between the volatility of rates and the level of rates. This has important implications for the choice of the model used by practitioners in financial markets.

More recently, a different approach to estimating these continuous time models, using a different discrete model, was put forward by Nowman (1997), who used Gaussian estimation econometric methods developed by Bergstrom (1983, 1985, 1986, 1990). The application of these Gaussian estimation methods has recently been demonstrated for these one-factor models by Nowman (1998, 2002) and Episcopos (2000).

Our main aim in this chapter is to apply these models to a recent set of data for an emerging market, namely the Czech Republic. We use daily interbank rates and find that the volatility of rates is highly dependent on the level of rates. The same thing was found in the CKLS study of the US market. The chapter is organized as follows: Section 2.2 outlines short-term interest rate models and the Gaussian estimation method. Section 2.3 describes the data. Empirical results are given in Section 2.4, and conclusions in Section 2.5.

2.2 Continuous time models and Gaussian estimation

Various models have been developed in the literature to model short-term interest rates. The features of interest rates that we would like to capture include a drift element and also the idea of mean reversion in interest rates. When rates happen to be high (low), they tend to revert to normal levels. The other important element to incorporate is any possible link between the level of rates and the volatility of rates. The CKLS model of short-term interest rates allows these important features to be incorporated in a general continuous time interest rate model:

$$dr(t) = \{\alpha + \beta r(t)\}dt + \sigma r^{\gamma}(t)\zeta(dt) \quad (t \geq 0) \tag{2.1}$$

where $\{r(t),\ t > 0\}$ is the short-term interest rate, α and β are the unknown drift and mean reversion structural parameters, σ is the volatility of the short-term rate, γ is the proportional volatility exponent and $\zeta(dt)$ is an error term. Various assumptions concerning the error term are used in the literature. Nowman (1997) used a general, weaker assumption based on the general theory of continuous time models developed in the seminal paper by Bergstrom (1983, Assumption 1). This allowed the error terms to be defined in a general manner, using random measure theory (see Bergstrom (1983) for full details).

Assumption 1 (Nowman, 1997): ζ is a random measure defined on all subsets of the half-line $0 < t < \infty$ with finite Lebesgue measure such that $E[\zeta(dt)] = 0$ and $E[\zeta(dt)^2] = dt$ and $E[\zeta(\Delta_1)\zeta(\Delta_2)] = 0$ for any disjoint sets Δ_1 and Δ_2 on the half-line $0 < t < \infty$.

The special cases of the CKLS model are given in Table 2.1. The first model in Table 2.1 is the general CKLS model. As can be seen, we obtain the other well-known models by imposing various assumptions on the parameters. The models of Merton (1973) and Vasicek (1977) assumed constant volatility $\gamma = 0$. In addition the Vasicek model incorporated mean reversion. The CIRSR model allowed a relationship between the volatility of rates and the square root of the rate level $\gamma = \frac{1}{2}$. The Dothan (1978), BR–SC and GBM models assumed a proportional relationship $\gamma = 1$. The CIRVR model assumed a higher value of $\gamma = \frac{3}{2}$. Lastly, the CEV model had a free parameter value γ.

Table 2.1 Continuous time interest rate models

Model		α	β	σ^2	γ
CKLS:	$dr(t) = \{\alpha + \beta r(t)\}dt + \sigma r^{\gamma}(t)\zeta(dt)$				
Merton:	$dr(t) = \alpha dt + \sigma\zeta(dt)$		0		0
Vasicek:	$dr(t) = \{\alpha + \beta r(t)\}dt + \sigma\zeta(dt)$				0
CIRSR:	$dr(t) = \{\alpha + \beta r(t)\}dt + \sigma r^{1/2}(t)\zeta(dt)$				$\frac{1}{2}$
Dothan:	$dr(t) = \sigma r(t)\zeta(dt)$	0	0		1
GBM:	$dr(t) = \beta r(t)dt + \sigma r(t)\zeta(dt)$	0			1
BR–SC:	$dr(t) = \{\alpha + \beta r(t)\}dt + \sigma r(t)\zeta(dt)$				1
CIRVR:	$dr(t) = \sigma r^{3/2}(t)\zeta(dt)$	0	0		$\frac{3}{2}$
CEV:	$dr(t) = \beta r(t)dt + \sigma r^{\gamma}(t)\zeta(dt)$	0			

In order to apply the Gaussian estimation methods of Bergstrom (1983, 1990), Nowman (1997) assumed, as an approximation to the true underlying model given by Equation 2.1, that over the interval $[0,T]$, $r(t)$ satisfied the stochastic differential equation

$$dr(t) = \{\alpha + \beta r(t)\}dt + \sigma\{r(t' - 1)\}^{\gamma}\zeta(dt) \tag{2.2}$$

where $t' - 1$ is the largest integer less than t. Nowman (1997) assumed in his Equation 2.2 that the volatility of interest rates changed at the beginning of the unit observation period and then remained constant. This assumption was made in order to use the Bergstrom (1983, 1984) formulation of general continuous time models (see Nowman (1997) for further details). In estimating the continuous time interest rate models, the problem we face is that the data are available only discretely.

Usually, we have interest rate data with a daily frequency to estimate the parameters of the model. The approach of Bergstrom (1983, 1984, 1990) is to derive from the solution of the continuous time model a discrete model in the form of a standard difference equation, the parameters of which are functions of the underlying parameters of the continuous time model. Such a discrete model is derived in Nowman (1997, Equations 4–6) based on Bergstrom (1984, theorem 2) but modified for the time-varying volatility element:

$$r(t) = e^{\beta}r(t-1) + \frac{\alpha}{\beta}(e^{\beta} - 1) + \eta_t \quad (t = 1,2, \ldots ,T) \tag{2.3}$$

$$E(\eta_s\eta_t) = 0 \quad (s \neq t) \tag{2.4}$$

$$\begin{aligned} E(\eta_t^2) &= \int_{t-1}^{t} e^{2(t-\tau)\beta}\sigma^2\{r(t-1)\}^{2\gamma}d\tau \\ &= \frac{\sigma^2}{2\beta}(e^{2\beta} - 1)\{r(t-1)\}^{2\gamma} = m_{tt}^2 \end{aligned} \tag{2.5}$$

Next we need to estimate the parameters. This is achieved using the function in Nowman (1997, equation 7), where $L(\theta)$ is defined as minus twice the logarithm of the Gaussian likelihood function with $\theta = [\alpha, \beta, \gamma, \sigma^2]$:

$$L(\theta) = \sum_{t=1}^{T}\left[2\log m_{tt} + \frac{\{r(t) - e^{\beta}r(t-1) - (\alpha/\beta)(e^{\beta} - 1)\}^2}{m_{tt}^2}\right] \tag{2.6}$$

Nowman (1997, equation 8) then defined the Gaussian likelihood function in the following form to obtain the Quasi Maximum Likelihood (QML) estimates:

$$L(\theta) = \sum_{t=1}^{T} [2 \log m_{tt} + \varepsilon_t^2] \tag{2.7}$$

where $\varepsilon_1, \ldots, \varepsilon_T$ are transformed residuals computed from $m_{tt}\, \varepsilon_t = \eta_t$. As a more formal check on the dynamic specification of each continuous time model, a Box–Pierce-type portmanteau test statistic proposed by Bergstrom (1990) can be used. This uses the vector of transformed residuals, which, if the model is correct, are independent and have variance 1. The statistic is given by

$$S = \frac{1}{n(T-l)} \sum_{i=1}^{l} \left(\sum_{t=l+1}^{T} \hat{\varepsilon}_t' \hat{\varepsilon}_{t-i} \right)^2$$

and is asymptotically distributed as χ^2 with l degrees of freedom and $n = 1$ (see Bergstrom (1990) for further details). In the empirical part we take $T = 3{,}127$ and $l = 12$.

2.3 The data

The interest rate used in this study is the daily one-month interbank rate extracted from the Datastream database over the period April 1992–April 2004, giving us a total of 3,127 observations. Table 2.2 shows the basic summary statistics. The average level of the one-month rate is 8.6 per cent, with a standard deviation of 4.7 per cent. The first six autocorrelations of the levels decay slowly, and the first differences

Table 2.2 Summary data statistics, April 1992–April 2004

Variable	Mean	SD	ρ_1	ρ_2	ρ_3	ρ_4	ρ_5	ρ_6	ADF
$r(t)$	8.6237	4.7735	0.99	0.98	0.98	0.97	0.97	0.96	−2.7326
$\Delta r(t)$	−0.0022	0.4898	−0.03	−0.01	0.16	−0.15	0.17	0.12	−18.998

Notes: Mean, standard deviations and autocorrelations of the daily interest rate in the Czech Republic. The variable $r(t)$ is the level and $\Delta r(t)$ is the daily change; ρ_j is the autocorrelation coefficient of order j. ADF denotes the augmented Dickey–Fuller unit root statistic.

are small. The augmented Dickey–Fuller unit root statistics do not reject the null hypothesis of a unit root in the level series.

2.4 Empirical results

In this section, we present in Table 2.3 the Gaussian estimates (standard errors in parentheses) of the CKLS model and its special cases. Following Nowman (1997), the explanatory power of each model is compared with that of the unrestricted model using the maximized Gaussian log-likelihood function value.

For the one-month rate based on the maximized Gaussian log-likelihood value, compared with the unrestricted model, the CEV model performs best. The results imply an unrestricted estimate of $\gamma = 1.9784$ for the one-month rate, thus indicating a significant volatility-level effect for this rate. This is in line with the results found in CKLS for the US market. There is no evidence of mean reversion in the one-month rate. Both CKLS and Nowman (1997) also found weak

Table 2.3 Gaussian estimates of continuous time models of the short-term interest rate: one-month interbank rate

Model	α	β	σ^2	γ	Log likelihood	χ^2 test	*df*	S-test
CKLS	−0.0001	0.0000*	0.1048	1.9784	18,179.127			22.2311
	(0.0000*)	(0.0007)	(0.0132)	(0.0235)				
Merton	0.0000*		0.0000*	0.0	15,069.701	6,218.852	2	518.743
	(0.0000*)		(0.0000*)					
Vasicek	0.0004	−0.0050	0.0000*	0.0	15,073.406	6,211.440	1	516.711
	(0.0001)	(0.0018)	(0.0000*)					
CIRSR	0.0001	−0.0006	0.0001	0.5	16,485.544	3,387.161	1	281.8539
	(0.0001)	(0.0012)	(0.0000*)					
Dothan			0.0010	1.0	17,438.809	1,480.636	3	107.786
			(0.0000*)					
GBM		−0.0001	0.0010	1.0	17,438.809	1,480.636	2	107.786
		(0.0001)	(0.0000*)					
BR–SC	−0.0001	0.0003	0.0010	1.0	17,438.966	1,480.322	1	107.716
	(0.0001)	(0.0010)	(0.0000*)					
CIRVR			0.0096	1.5	17,994.477	369.300	3	42.7565
			(0.0002)					
CEV		−0.0005	0.1053	1.9791	18,178.814	0.6260	1	22.1944
		(0.0003)	(0.0141)	(0.0250)				

Notes: 0.0000* denotes numbers $< 10^{-4}$. The critical values at the 5% and 1% significance levels for the χ^2 test are 21.03 and 26.29, respectively.

evidence of mean reversion. Based on the χ^2 likelihood ratio test under the null hypothesis that the nested model's restrictions are valid, the results imply that we can reject all models except the CEV model. Turning to the *S*-statistic values, the results imply that we can reject most models apart from the CKLS and CEV models.

2.5 Conclusions

In this chapter, we have applied a number of well-known continuous time models of short-term interest rates to an emerging market, namely, the Czech Republic. Using daily data of one-month interbank rates, we estimated the CKLS model and eight special cases using the general Gaussian estimation method of Nowman (1997). We found that the volatility of rates is highly dependent on the level of rates, as has been found in the US market, and that the CEV model performed the best. This has implications in terms of the choice of the most appropriate model to be used in this financial market for the purpose of pricing financial assets.

References

Bergstrom, A. R. (1983), Gaussian estimation of structural parameters in higher-order continuous time dynamic models, *Econometrica* 51, 117–52.

Bergstrom, A. R. (1985), The estimation of parameters in nonstationary higher-order continuous time dynamic models, *Econometric Theory* 1, 369–85.

Bergstrom, A. R. (1986), The estimation of open higher-order continuous time dynamic models with mixed stock and flow data, *Econometric Theory* 2, 350–73.

Bergstrom, A. R. (1990), Continuous time econometric modelling, Oxford University Press, Oxford.

Brennan, M. J. and E. S. Schwartz (1980), Analyzing convertible bonds, *Journal of Financial and Quantitative Analysis* 15, 907–29.

Chan, K. C., G. A. Karolyi, F. A. Longstaff and A. B. Sanders (1992), An empirical comparison of alternative models of the short-term interest rate, *Journal of Finance* 47, 1209–27.

Cox, J. C. (1975), Notes on option pricing 1: constant elasticity of variance diffusion, Working Paper, Stanford University.

Cox, J. C. and S. Ross (1976), The valuation of options for alternative stochastic processes, *Journal of Financial Economics* 3, 145–66.

Cox, J. C., J. E. Ingersoll, and S. Ross (1980), An analysis of variable rate loan contracts, *Journal of Finance* 35, 389–403.

Cox, J. C., J. E. Ingersoll, and S. Ross (1985), A theory of the term structure of interest rates, *Econometrica* 53, 385–407.
Dahlquist, M. (1996), On alternative interest rate processes, *Journal of Banking and Finance* 20, 1093–119.
Dothan, U. L. (1978), On the term structure of interest rates, *Journal of Financial Economics* 6, 59–69.
Episcopos, A. (2000), Further evidence on alternative continuous time models of the short-term interest rate, *Journal of International Financial Markets, Institutions and Money* 10, 199–212.
Hiraki, T and N. Takezawa (1997), How sensitive is short-term Japanese interest rate volatility to the level of the interest rate? *Economic Letters* 56, 325–32.
Merton, R. C. (1973), Theory of rational option pricing, *Bell Journal of Economics and Management Science* 4, 141–83.
Nowman, K. B. (1997), Gaussian estimation of single-factor continuous time models of the term structure of interest rates, *Journal of Finance* 52, 1695–706.
Nowman, K. B. (1998), Continuous time short rate interest rate models, *Applied Financial Economics* 8, 401–7.
Nowman, K. B. (2002), The volatility of Japanese interest rates: evidence for certificate of deposit and gensaki rates, *International Review of Financial Analysis* 11, 29–38.
Tse, Y. K. (1995), Some international evidence on the stochastic behaviour of interest rates, *Journal of International Money and Finance* 14, 721–38.
Vasicek, O. (1977), An equilibrium characterization of the term structure, *Journal of Financial Economics* 5, 177–88.

3

Excess Credit Risk and Banks' Default Risk: An Application of Default Prediction Models to Banks in Emerging Market Economies

Christophe J. Godlewski

3.1 Introduction and literature survey

The last 20 years have witnessed several bank failures throughout the world, particularly in emerging market economies (EMEs) (Bell and Pain, 2000). The interest in bank failures comes mainly from their costs: financial losses for the stakeholders (shareholders, clients and deposit insurance funds), loss of competitiveness and potential destabilization of the financial system via contagion mechanisms, whereby several individual failures lead to a banking crisis. The resolution of these failures is a waste of resources, which are particularly scarce in EMEs (Honohan, 1997).[1]

Excess credit risk and bad corporate governance in banks are the principal internal default factors.

A study by the Office of the Comptroller of the Currency (OCC, 1988) lists the characteristics of failed banks in the United States of America during the 1980s. The main cause of failure was the bad quality of bank assets. This quality is the responsibility of banks' managers; therefore, inefficient risk management was at the heart of bank default. The four main factors behind bank failures were

- inadequate credit policy,
- an inadequate system of control and monitoring,

- an inadequate system for identifying non-performing loans (NPLs),
- excessive concentration of decisionmaking authority.

In a recent review of the principal banking crisis factors, Llellewyn (2002) points out five common characteristics throughout the world:

- an inefficient process for risk analysis, management and control,
- insufficient monitoring,
- a perverse or weak incentives structure,
- insufficient information transfer,
- inadequate corporate governance.

Bad risk management and control generate excess risk in banks. This excess risk is the output of a credit decision that increases banks' default risk to a higher level than what stakeholders would want. The main cause for such credit risk-taking behaviour is the fact that the agent who is responsible for the credit decision does not bear all the costs of the decision.

Different symptoms of excess credit risk can be found in the literature (see Keeton and Morris, 1987; Clair, 1992; Honohan, 1997):

- a low-quality loans portfolio (a high ratio of NPLs),
- high concentration of loans in the portfolio (by term, borrower, industrial and/or geographic sector, type of debt instrument),
- over optimistic evaluation of borrower's quality,
- insufficient risk pricing,
- high correlations between loans (different type of loans and NPLs),
- excessive loans growth,
- absorption of risk above bank's technical capacity.

Concerning the relationship between the control of the agent and his risk taking behaviour, Gorton and Rosen (1995) put forward an explanation of bank default in the United States of America based on inefficient corporate governance mechanisms, which favours excess risk.

Wage policy is one of the internal corporate governance mechanisms which are supposed to resolve agency costs problem[2] (Jensen, 1993). The agent's salary (the manager responsible for the credit decision and risk taking) is indexed on his performance. He also gets shares in the bank's capital (e.g. stock-options).[3] Following Gorton and Rosen (1995), excessive risk taking incentives depend on the level of insider's shares. In a declining industry, where good investment opportunities become scarce,[4] bad managers-insiders can preserve their jobs and increase their revenues allocating loans to risky borrowers. This relationship between risk taking and the level of managerial holdings is non-linear and concave. For majority holdings, the device is efficient because it disciplines the manager (in case of excess risk and bank default, he loses his human capital investment and his shares), thereby reducing the incentives for excessive risk taking even in a declining banking industry. For minority holdings, the manager keeps his ability to resist the shareholder's control (entrenchment), while still receiving the revenues of his shares, through excess risk, which is unobservable by the principal (shareholder). This explanation of excess risk is particularly relevant in the case of banks in EME, where managers and executives often hold shares in banks.

The results of empirical studies on the impact of ownership structure on risk taking in banks provide mixed evidence. Saunders *et al.* (1990) find that banks controlled by a majority of shareholders-outsiders are less risky. On the contrary, Knopf and Teall (1996) and Anderson and Fraser (2000) find that banks controlled by a majority of managers-insiders are more risky. Demsetz *et al.* (1997) find that this is particularly significant in low charter value banks.

We can notice other bank default factors, which we can call external. These are macroeconomic and market structure factors. Other default factors are regulatory and institutional ones.

The main macroeconomic default factors are generally also those which cause banking crisis, particularly in EMEs. These factors are, among others, high inflation, interest rate fluctuations, volatility of foreign capital flows, an inadequate exchange rate regime and public debt (see Caprio and Klingebiel, 1996; Goldstein and Turner, 1996; Gonzalez-Hermosillo, 1999; Demirgüç-Kunt and Detragiarche, 2000). The structural and regulatory change in EMEs increase the probability of these macroeconomic default factors. The banks can't correctly evaluate the riskiness of their borrowers in a changing economic environment. A boom and bust cycle can emerge.

A hard competition on the credit market can push the bank to accept 'bad risks', offering debt contract's conditions which do not reflect the riskiness of the counterpart (or which do not follow the bank's credit policy), particularly no risk adjusted pricing. Keeley (1990) focuses on the relationship between risk taking and charter value. This charter value is more important when the bank has monopoly power on the market. The threat of losing charter value disciplines the bank's risk-taking behaviour. Following the deregulation of banking activities in the United States of America during the 1980s, the market power of banks eroded, and their charter value decreased. Meanwhile, the banks had to increase their efforts in order to keep their profits at a certain level. This has generated excessive risk taking incentives.

Saunders and Wilson (2001) extended Keeley's work, studying the sensibility of the relationship between risk taking and charter value to economic cycles. They find that charter value is procyclical. It increases in periods of economic expansion, and decreases in periods of recession. Therefore, the disciplining effect of charter value is reduced when the economic environment becomes adverse.

Some theoretical models have also investigated this relationship between excess risk and competition. Hellmann *et al.* (2000) find that excessive risk taking can appear in a highly competitive market. Banking regulation can alter this effect, but generates its own adverse incentives. Covitz and Heitfeld (1999), Cordella and Yeyati (2002) and Repullo (2004) find similar results.

Excess risk incentives can also have their sources in the characteristics of the banking regulation, like the deposits insurance system with fixed prime, or the regulator's behaviour.

The existence of a guarantee fund which insures deposits reduces the depositor's incentives to monitor the bank and therefore reduces market discipline. The fixed insurance prime incites the bank to use deposits to finance risky credits and can generate excess risk.

The regulator's behaviour generates some regulatory discipline.[5] This discipline is imperfect because of specific problems like too big to fail (TBTF) and forbearance Kane (1989). Regulator's forbearance is a non-intervention in a problem bank. This kind of behaviour can lead to a more costly default of the bank, compared to an earlier intervention. It can also generate adverse incentives for the remaining banks, which adopt excessive risk taking behaviour. The TBTF problem is the result of conflict of interests between the bank and the regulator, and is also a consequence of the forbearance problem. Big banks that default would generate important economic costs (losses for the stakeholders, destabilization of financial systems, etc.)[6] and anticipate non-intervention of the regulator in case of insolvability. These banks can engage themselves in excessive risk-taking behaviour.

The intertemporal aspect of bank's capital regulation can incite it to excess risk (e.g. Koehn and Santomero, 1980; Kim and Santomero, 1988; Blum, 1999). The regulatory obligation to hold a minimum level of regulatory capital buffer in period $t + 1$ puts pressure on the bank's profits in period t. The regulation being costly and thereby reducing the expected profits and charter value, the bank can be incited to generate the additional revenues by increasing risk taking.

Regulatory and institutional environment's characteristics can also generate excessive risk taking incentives.

The work of La Porta *et al.* (1997, 1998, 2000) put forward the impact of the institutional environment's quality on the protection of stakeholders (protection of investors from insiders' expropriation), and on the nature and efficiency of capital markets and the performance of financial systems. The laws which govern the relationship between the stakeholder (principal) and the manager (agent) are affected by the country's institutional environment. This environment is a crucial determinant of the efficiency of corporate governance mechanisms which rule the principal–agent relationship. It can also favour excess risk or reduce the efficiency of its control by other mechanisms and institutions.

Klapper and Love (2002) study the relationship between corporate governance system and institutional environment in 14 EMEs. They use governance indicators from Crédit Lyonnais Securities Asia (CLSA).[7] Their results confirm the presence of weak governance in weak institutional and regulatory environments. This relationship affects negatively the firm's performance. Mitton (2002) finds that inefficient governance mechanisms[8] have weakened firms and contributed to amplify the Asian Flu. Hussain and Wihlborg (1999) also find that institutional factors have deepened the Asian Crisis, and the insolvency procedures have amplified its length.

Barth *et al.* (2001) study the relationship between bank regulation and supervision and banking industry performance. Their results put forward the role of market discipline as a crucial element of regulatory and supervision strategy. This form of discipline seems to be most efficient in monitoring bank's behaviour. Barth *et al.* (2000)

focus on the relationship between different systems of regulatory and types of ownership structure, and performances and stability of banks. Their results show that regulatory restrictions of banking activities affect the whole industry negatively. The more a market is contestable the more is market discipline efficient, and can restrict bank behaviour to be more conservative. Calomiris and Powell (2000) find similar results in their study of regulatory evolution in Argentina during the 1990s. This evolution was mainly based on enhancing market discipline, and incited banks to manage their risks more conservatively, which is a difficult task after a period of financial liberalization. Barth *et al.* (2002) extend this analysis and compare the impact of different supervisory systems on bank profitability. The impact seems to be weak. A unique supervisory body would increase a bank's profitability.

As we have seen, several bank default factors emerge from the literature. However, the impact of institutional factors (regulation, rule of law) on fundamental internal determinants of default – excess risk – remains neglected.

The purpose of this chapter is to study the role of the institutional factors in driving excessive risk taking. Therefore, we adopt a two-step approach (Maddala, 1983) inspired from Demirgüç-Kunt (1989b) and Thomson (1992), and we apply it to a database on EME's banks which contains accounting, regulatory and institutional information (La Porta *et al.*, 1997, 1998; Bankscope, Barth *et al.*, 2001). The rest of this chapter is organized as follows. We survey the literature on predicting bank default's modelling in Section 3.2, where we also present our approach. Our data and main results are presented in Section 3.3. We conclude the study in Section 3.4.

3.2 Models of bank default prediction

Several empirical studies on bank default prediction's models (or early warning signal, EWS, models) using single equation appeared during the 1970s, mainly in the United States of America (see Demirgüç-Kunt, 1989a, for a detailed survey). At the end of the 1980s, two equation models appeared. Their objective was to dissociate the internal and external factors of default, and especially to distinguish the insolvency factors from the regulatory failure factors.

The most frequent time horizon used in EWS models is one year. The definition of default concerns difficulties affecting a bank's solvency. Default banks are called problem banks.

3.2.1 Single-equation EWS models

The EWS models are supposed to translate different banks' performance and solvency indicators into default risk estimation.[9] Using this estimation, the regulator can discriminate between more- or less-risky banks. Early identification of problem banks helps to initiate preventive and corrective actions. Much of a bank's default explanation and prediction models are based on CAMEL typology. This typology uses five risk factors[10] which form a bank's soundness rating.[11]

Sinkey (1975) was the first to study problem banks, applying a multivariate discriminant analysis (MDA) to a sample of 220 small American commercial banks, of which 110 defaults for the period 1969–72. From 100 ratios, Sinkey chose 10 of which 6 were significant. The quality of bank assets is the most significant factor. Other discriminant variables are assets' composition, loans' characteristics, capital adequacy, sources and use of income, efficiency and profitability.

Altman *et al.* (1977) also applied an MDA model to a sample of 212 American savings and deposits banks for the period 1966–73. They divided their sample into three sub-samples: problem banks (56), fragile banks (having temporary problems) (49) and healthy banks (107). From 32 tested ratios, 7 were significant. The most discriminant variable was the operational profit and its evolution.

Martin (1977) was the first to use a logit model. He studied a sample of 5,642 healthy banks and 58 failed banks for the period 1970–76. After testing 25 ratios, 4 were significant, mainly the capital asset ratio, and the loans portfolio's composition to total assets ratio.

Avery and Hanweck (1984), Barth *et al.* (1985) and Benston (1985) have also contributed to the EWS models literature, applying logit models to different samples of banks (respectively, 1,290 of which 100 were defaults, 906 of which 318 were defaults, and 890 of which 178 were defaults) for various periods during the early 1980s, exclusively in the United States. Generally less than 10 ratios were significant. These were mainly proxies of the loans portfolio composition and quality, capital ratio and the sources of income.

Pantalone and Platt (1987) proposed a model which included most of the CAMEL proxies: profitability, management's efficiency, leverage, diversification and economic environment. They used a sample of 113 defaults and 226 healthy banks from the early 1980s. Their results confirmed that the main cause of default was bad credit risk management, which occurred due to excess risk and/or inefficient risk taking, control and monitoring.

Barr and Siems (1994) proposed two new EWS models, with a two-year time horizon. Their model included CAMEL proxies and efficiency scores[12] as management's quality proxies (the M is the most difficult CAMEL-type risk factor to estimate objectively), and a proxy of the economic conditions. They followed the finding of Barr *et al.* (1993), that efficiency scores decreased three years before bank's default.[13] This sensibility was very useful for management's quality estimation in EWS models. Barr and Siems applied the probit model integrating efficiency scores obtained from a Data Envelopment Analysis methodology as management's quality proxies, with four other CAMEL proxy variables. Their model was more robust and precise than the Martin (1977) and Pantalone and Platt (1987) models.

3.2.2 Two equation models with institutional factors

Two equation models allow to dissociate risk factors that affect bank solvency from external factors (particularly regulatory ones) and drive the regulator's behaviour, especially his propensity to intervene in problem banks.

Gajewski (1988) was the first to incorporate such a distinction between insolvency and failure in his model, studying a sample of 2,447 healthy and 134 default banks. Gajewski (1988) used two equations: the first models economic insolvency and the second, administrative failure. After testing 25 ratios, 10 were significant.

Following the work of Kane (1989), Demirgüç-Kunt (1989b) also proposed to treat economic insolvency as one of the factors influencing regulator's decision to intervene and declare a bank failed, apart from other economic, political and bureaucratic factors.[14] In the same spirit, Thomson (1992) proposed to model the failure decision of the regulator as a call option. He supposes a distinction between insolvency and failure, the latter being a regulatory and administrative decision. His model builds from two equations: the first models the net value of the bank (solvency), the second models the bank's failure (allowing to model the regulator's behaviour). Demirgüç-Kunt's (1989b) approach was very similar.[15] Both studies apply a two-step method following Maddala (1983), estimating the first equation with the ordinary least square method (OLS) and the second one with a logit model.

3.2.3 The two-step model: a proposition

Our main objective is to study the impact of regulatory and institutional factors of EMEs on excessive risk taking incentives. A two-step approach allows a distinction between regulatory and institutional factors and excess risk, from the relationship between this internal default factor and other default factors.

In our study, the indicator of excess risk is the *ratio of non performing loans*, NPL/GL, which we discretize in order to obtain our first dependent polytomic variable of three classes, CNPL.

It is built as follows:

$$\text{CNPL} = \begin{cases} 1 & \text{If NPL/GL} < 5\% \quad \text{(low excess risk)} \\ 2 & \text{If } 5\% < \text{NPL/GL} < 20\% \quad \text{(medium excess risk)} \\ 3 & \text{If NPL/GL} > 20\% \quad \text{(high excess risk).} \end{cases}$$

Our second dependent variable is a dummy, DEFAULT, which is equal to 1 if the bank was in default at time t.[16]

The two steps of our approach are:

1. estimation of the relation between an indicator of excess risk CNPL and regulatory and institutional factors using an ordered logit model;
2. estimation of a bank default function integrating the estimated value $\widehat{\text{CNPL}}$ and other risk factors using a binary logit model.

The two equations to be estimated are:[17]

$$\log\left(\frac{p(\text{CNPL})}{1 - p(\text{CNPL})}\right) = \gamma + x_i'\varphi + \xi_i \tag{3.1}$$

$$\log\left(\frac{p(\text{DEFAULT})}{1 - p(\text{DEFAULT})}\right) = \alpha + y_i'\beta + \varepsilon_i \tag{3.2}$$

and X_i' = regulatory and institutional factors, and $Y_i' = \widehat{\text{CNPL}}$ and the other risk factors, the residuals ξ_i and ε_i having logistic distributions.

The variables used to estimate Equation 3.1 are defined in Table 3.1. The first seven regulatory variables come from Barth *et al.* (2001) database, the last institutional variable from La Porta *et al.* (1997, 1998). We have selected the most representative variable of different dimensions of the regulatory and institutional environment in studied EMEs.

The variables in Equation 3.2 are respectively $\widehat{CNPL}$, which is the estimated value of the excess risk indicator from Equation 3.1, and six proxy variables for risk factors (see Table 3.2).

Table 3.1 Explanatory regulatory and institutional variables used in Equation 3.1

Variables	**Definition**
Regulatory proxies	
PHOLDEM	Equals 1 if the first holding of the bank comes from an EME (38.14% of our sample)
MCAR	Minimum regulatory capital ratio (m. 9.31, SD 1.34, min and max 8 and 11.5, respectively)
DEPOSITINS	Equals 1 if a deposits insurance system exists (78.13% of our sample)
FREQEXAM	Equals 1 (2) if large banks are examined on-site once (twice) a year (86.93% and 13.07% of our sample)
MISCMGTREP	Equals 1 if the auditor has the legal obligation to report management/executive mismanagement (45.8% of our sample)
LEGALACT	Equals 1 if the regulator can use legal actions against the auditors for neglected work (88.03% of our sample)
PROHIBABL	Equals 1 if abroad loan making is prohibited by banking regulation (13.89% of our sample)
Institutional proxies	
RULEOFLAW	Rule of law quality's indicator (m. 4.95, SD 1.65, min and max 2.08 and 6.78, respectively)
LEGSYSFR	Equals 1 if the legal system is based on the French system (81.1% of our sample)

Sources: Bankscope, Barth *et al.* (2001) and La Porta *et al.* (1997, 1998).

Table 3.2 CAMEL-type explanatory risk factors used in Equation 3.2

Variables	Definition	CAMEL category
EQTA	Equity/total assets	C
EQTL	Equity/total loans	C
TA	Total assets	A
NPLGL	Non-performing loans/ gross loans	A
NLTA	Net loans/total assets	A
LLRGL	Loan losses reserves/ gross loans	A
PEXP	Personal expenses/ total operating expenses	M
NI	Net income	E
NIM	Net interest margin	E
ROA	Net income/total assets	E
TDTA	Total deposits/total assets	L
LIQATA	Liquid assets/total assets	L
TLTD	Total loans/total deposits	L

Source: Bankscope.

3.3 Data and results

3.3.1 Data

We have built a bank defaults database in most of the EMEs from three geographic zones: Asia, Latin America and Central and Eastern Europe. Three arguments motivate our choice of these countries:

- the important number of bank defaults in these countries during the 1990s,
- heavier consequences of bank failure in these countries,
- interconnection and globalization of financial and banking systems expose developed economies to heavier difficulties in case of defaults in EMEs.

In order to build our database, we have contacted local regulatory institutions.[18] We have also used information from the on-line database Banker's Almanac (www.bankersalmanac.com). It helps us to identify the name and the time of default.

We consider as default a bank which cannot operate without external support, or which is already engaged in a procedure which leads to its exit from the market. Therefore, a bank is in default when it is under one of the following procedures:

- external administration (regulatory and restructuring agency support[19]),
- banking licence suspension or revocation,
- liquidation,
- failure.

Following this typology, we found 297 defaults for the period 1990–2002 for 34 EMEs. Keeping only commercial, savings and investment banks, and dropping years where residual defaults occurred, we finally got a database of 270 default banks for which we have accounting data from Bankscope.[20] There were 24 defaults in 1997, 80 in 1998, 75 in 1999, 37 in 2000, 36 in 2001 and 18 in 2002, respectively.

We then completed our database with accounting (balance sheet) and governance (ownership structure) data from Bankscope. Accounting data concern details of balance sheet and profit and loss positions. These data are annual and denominated in thousands of US dollars. They allow us to build CAMEL ratio (Table 3A.1) proxies – the risk factors of Equation 3.2. The governance data give us information concerning the first holding's nationality, the holdings percentage and their names.

We also included regulatory and institutional variables from Barth *et al.* (2001) database (available on-line on www.worldbank.org) acquired by them through interviews with local regulatory institutions, and institutional information from La Porta *et al.* (1997, 1998) database. These data are mainly qualitative and are grouped by country. La Porta *et al.* dataset contains various indicators and dummies reflecting the quality of institutional and governance environments. The focus is put on stakeholders' rights protection mechanisms.

We have first studied descriptive statistics of different balance sheet ratios, particularly their means for the state default versus non-default. These statistics were aberrant for small default banks, indicating that other factors were at play at the source of their problems (probably macroeconomic ones). We have therefore bounded the variable *total assets* (TA) in order to eliminate small banks (TA above the first quartile equal to US$105.11 million). A first size criterion determines our sample. We then focused on banks whose main activity is credit allocation, and therefore the main source of risk is credit risk, and we have bounded the variables *net loans in total assets*, NLTA (elimination of the first percentile equal to 25.32 per cent of total assets) and *Total Deposits to Total Assets*, TDTA (elimination of the first 5 per cent equal to 26.81 per cent of total assets). A second bank's activity criterion determines our sample.

We finally got a pooled sample of 894 banks for the period 1996–2002, of which 61 were defaults. Commercial banks compose the main part of our sample (more than 95 per cent of our sample). The majority of the defaults occurred in 1997 and 1998, respectively, 23 and 17, and then there were 4, 9 and 7 in the following years: 1999, 2000 and 2001.

Table 3.3 shows the frequencies of default by country. Table 3.4 shows descriptive statistics for the main balance sheet variables and ratios (in millions US dollars, the ratios are in percentages).

Table 3.3 Default frequency by country

Country	**Defaults**	**Banks**	**Def. freq.**
Argentina	7	151	4.64
Bolivia	7	23	30.43
Colombia	3	104	2.88
Ecuador	2	63	3.17
Indonesia	1	68	1.47
Korea (South)	12	33	36.36
Mexico	2	95	2.11
Malaysia	19	82	23.17
Peru	4	100	4
Thailand	3	54	5.56
Venezuela	1	121	0.8
	61	894	6.82

Def. freq.: In sample default frequency.

Source: Author's bank default database.

Table 3.4 Descriptive statistics of the main balance sheet variables and ratios

Variables	*N*	Mean	SD	Min	Max
Default					
TA	61	5,053.76	8,211.61	108.3	35,254.67
NI	61	−144.2	490.74	−3,203.08	164.66
ROA	61	−4.62	17.52	−112.21	2.06
NLTA	61	60.36	12.65	26.78	90.79
TDTA	61	79.79	11.74	38.4	99.34
EQTA	61	4.77	18.62	−120.92	28.26
EQTL	61	8.05	35.5	−221.93	59.3
LLRGL	61	7.88	11.05	1.19	60.24
NPLGL	61	16.66	13.64	1.83	65.72
PEXP	61	27.29	12.54	1.12	54.75
NIM	61	2.76	7.71	−52.99	13.15
LIQATA	61	18	8.82	4.88	42.87
TLTD	61	76.77	16.02	29.11	124.1
Non-default					
TA	833	3,366.76	7,110	106.7	56,740.29
NI	833	−13.45	209.54	−2,461.5	880.32
ROA	833	0.62	3.56	−35.15	23.66
NLTA	833	56.8	13.74	25.38	92.35
TDTA	833	75.92	12.66	18.51	95.19
EQTA	833	11.25	6.65	−15.25	53.45
EQTL	833	21.28	13.76	−31.93	100.98
LLRGL	833	6.63	5.65	0	50.56
NPLGL	833	10.68	11.23	0	89.59
PEXP	833	33.44	12.44	0.29	76.96
NIM	833	8.2	7.67	−8.06	55.8
LIQATA	833	23.24	13.35	0.34	69.08
TLTD	833	77.36	27.02	27.68	362.93

N: number of observations; SD: standard deviation; Min: minimum; Max: maximum.

Source: Bankscope.

3.3.2 Results

We ran two regressions corresponding to two different specifications in order to estimate Equation 3.1:

1. regression 3.1.1 with proxy variables of the regulatory environment (Barth *et al.*, 2001);
2. regression 3.1.2 with proxy variables of the regulatory environment (Barth *et al.*, 2001) and proxy variables of the institutional environment (La Porta *et al.*, 1997, 1998).

Our results are shown in Table 3.5.[21] We then ran two regressions of the CAMEL-type logit model (Equation 3.2) including the estimated values of $\widehat{\text{CNPL}}$ (from regressions 3.1.1 and 3.1.2) as dependent variables to explain default (regressions 3.2.1 and 3.2.2). Table 3.6 presents our results.[22] Table 3.7 presents the results of a binary CAMEL-type logit model, for comparison.[23]

Table 3.5 Estimation results of the excess credit risk Equation 3.1

Variables	**3.1.1**	**3.1.2**
PHOLDEM	0.506***	0.701***
	(0.16)	(0.16)
MCAR	0.091***	0.359***
	(0.03)	(0.08)
DEPOSITINS	0.668***	
	(0.22)	
FREQEXAM	1.157***	1.16***
	(0.23)	(0.24)
MISCMGTREP	0.527***	0.579**
	(0.19)	(0.24)
LEGALACT	1.652***	
	(0.29)	
PROHIBABL	1.661***	1.035***
	(0.25)	(0.24)
RULEOFLAW		0.448***
		(0.1)
LEGSYSFR		2.051***
		(0.35)
N	727	704
χ^2	510.31***	475.56***
Log *L*	−648.03	−638.88
% concordant	71.30%	70.10%

Intercepts significant but not shown.
N: number of observations; Log *L*: logarithm of the likelihood; % concordant: percentage of concordant reclassification.
*** and ** significant at 1% and 5% level, respectively.

Table 3.6 Estimation results of the default risk Equation 3.2

Variables	3.2.1	Marginal effect	m. elasticity	3.2.2	Marginal effect	m. elasticity
$\widehat{\text{CNPL}}$	2.266**	0.161	0.174	1.969*	0.142	0.155
	(0.93)			(1.01)		
EQTL	−0.025**	−0.00178	−0.168	−0.025**	−0.0018	−0.169
	(0.01)			(0.01)		
PEXP	−0.005	–	–	−0.003	–	–
	(0.01)			(0.01)		
NIM	0.215***	−0.0153	−0.407	−0.2***	−0.0144	−0.383
	(0.05)			(0.05)		
LIQATA	0.048***	−0.00341	−0.38	0.048***	−0.00346	−0.4
	(0.01)			(0.01)		
TLTD	−0.007*	−0.0005	−0.219	−0.006*	−0.00043	−0.203
	(0.004)			(0.004)		
N. def.	56			55		
N	727			704		
χ^2	676.98***			648.94***		
Log *L*	−165.43			−163.51		
McFadden R^2	67.17%			67.10%		
Def. reclas. rate	83.90%			87.30%		

Intercept not significant and not shown.
m. elasticity: mean elasticity; *N*: number of observations; *N*. def.: number of defaults; Log *L*: logarithm of the likelihood; Def. reclas. rate: defaults correct reclassification rate. ***, ** and * significant at 1%, 5% and 10% level, respectively.

3.3.3 Discussion

First holding from an EMEs (PHOLDEM) has a positive impact on excess risk. We can explain this result by the fact that the state often remains the first holding in EMEs. It does not discipline and monitor correctly and efficiently the risk-taking behaviour of banks (forbearance, anticipation of intervention in case of difficulties). The knowledge transfer, particularly the art of risk management, is also less important as with a first holding from a developed country.

A higher minimal regulatory capital ratio (MCAR) increases excess risk. Generally this ratio is higher in EMEs (closer to 12 per cent than to 8 per cent), in order to limit excess risk and to force banks to recapitalize, and become more solvent and sound. However, as we have seen, a higher regulatory capital can incite banks to take excess risk,

Table 3.7 Estimation results of a binary logit default model (CAMEL-type risk factors only)

Variables	CAMEL (3.2.1)	Marginal effect	m. elasticity
EQTL	−0.022*	−0.00156	−0.157
	(0.01)		
NPLGL	0.002	0.00014	0.011
	(0.01)		
PEXP	0.002	0.00014	0.023
	(0.01)		
NIM	−0.172***	−0.0122	−0.346
	(0.05)		
LIQATA	−0.048***	−0.00341	−0.377
	(0.02)		
TLTD	−0.005***	−0.00036	−0.154
	(0.01)		
N. def.	56		
N	727		
χ^2	671.50***		
Log *L*	−168.17		
McFadden R^2	66.63%		
Def. reclass. rate	78.60%		

Intercept not significant and not shown.
m. elasticity: mean elasticity; *N*: number of observations; *N*. def.: number of defaults; Log *L*: logarithm of the likelihood; def. reclas. rate: defaults correct reclassification rate.
*** and * significant at 1% and 5% level, respectively.

as additional capital implies additional efforts in terms of profitability, which can be achieved by increasing risk taking.

The existence of a deposits insurance system (DEPOSITINS) reduces excess risk. This result seems counter-intuitive concerning the moral hazard problem which is a consequence of such a system. However, such a guarantee fund protects depositors, and can therefore reduce excess risk needed to generate more profits, in order to signal good performances and to avoid liquidity problems.

The frequency of on-site exams (FREQEXAM) reduces excess risk, thereby producing some regulatory discipline. The threat of a frequent exam which can result in licence suspension or revocation (and charter value elimination) in case of nonconformity to regulatory standards can incite the bank to adopt a more conservative risk-taking behaviour.

Auditor's reports on mismanagement (MISCMGTREP) have a positive effect on excess risk in the first regression 3.1.1 and a negative effect in the second one 3.1.2. We were expecting a negative sign of this coefficient, because such a report can be the basis for an ulterior regulatory intervention. Without the institutional variables (RULEOFLAW and LEGSYSFR), the sign is positive, signalling either that this type of threat is not credible (auditor's negligence for example), or that such reports have an adverse effect, inciting bank managers to a 'maximum' level of excess risk before a probable regulator's intervention after a negative report on mismanagement. In the second regression 3.1.2 the sign is negative, indicating a disciplining effect of the auditor's report, controlling for the quality of the country's rule of law.

Legal action against negligent auditors (LEGALACT) has a negative impact on excess risk. Through disciplining auditors, the regulator can affect bank's incentives, because its excessive risk taking will be found out easily if audits are done more efficiently.

Foreign loans prohibitions (PROHIBABL) that have a positive impact on excess risk, because such regulation reduces loans portfolio diversification opportunities (Allen and Gale, 2000).[24]

These results clearly exhibit the existing complementarity of regulating factors that enforce market discipline, which is considered to be an inherent part of the corporate governance mechanism (Jensen, 1993). These factors also have a positive effect on regulatory discipline. Our results show the importance of institutional environment in enhancing the efficiency of other corporate governance mechanisms as well, thereby reducing excessive risk-taking incentives. Referring to our results, bank regulation has a significant impact on excess risk in EME banks. This impact can be adverse, as with minimum regulatory capital (MCAR). However, regulatory discipline seems to be efficient, curbing excessive risk-taking incentives.

Taking into account the correlations, we have dropped variables DEPOSITINS and LEGALACT in regression 3.1.2 in order to include variables RULEOFLAW and LEGSYSFR. The most significant variable is RULEOFLAW and it is the least correlated with other explicative variables of our model (compared to other indicators of stakeholders and debt holders' rights protection). It allows us also to include a proxy of rule of law quality and test its impact on excess risk. Variable

LEGSYSFR has been introduced to control the legal system's origin (dummy variables of British and German legal systems were correlated with other explicative variables of our model). The signs of these two-institutional variables are negative, indicating that excess risk is reduced in a state of law. The French legal origin has a significant impact. The impact of institutional factors on excess risk is significant. An institutional environment of quality reduces excessive risk-taking incentives.

When we introduce the variable $\widehat{\text{CNPL}}$ in our model of bank default prediction (Equation 3.2), and after controlling other CAMEL risk-factor variables, we find that only proxies of risk factor C, E and L are significant with coherent signs. The marginal effect of $\widehat{\text{CNPL}}$ is the most important, indicating that the default probability is highly sensitive to $\widehat{\text{CNPL}}$, and therefore to institutional factors which affect excess risk. This variable contributes the most to default probability. In terms of elasticity, a 1 per cent increase of variables NIM or LIQUIDASSET reduces more default probability (respectively, 40.7 and 38.3 per cent in regression 3.2.1, and 38 and 40 per cent in regression 3.2.2). The elasticity of $\widehat{\text{CNPL}}$ is the lowest (17.4 and 15.5 per cent, respectively). It seems that banks in EMEs of our sample should concentrate more on margin and assets liquidity to reduce their default probability.

We remark that default reclassification rates are better when we use our two-step approach, with the integration of the estimated excess risk indicator $\widehat{\text{CNPL}}$ from equation 3.1 (83.9 and 87.3 per cent, respectively),[25] compared to those from a CAMEL binary logit model (78.64 per cent). The default reclassification rate derived from our specification including institutional variables (regression 3.1.2) is the highest. The default reclassification rates derived from CAMEL binary logit models including the same regulatory and institutional (Table 3A.3, regressions CAMEL 1 and CAMEL 2) remains low (82.1 and 81.6 per cent, respectively).

3.4 Conclusion

Risk-taking behaviour in banks can be affected by the regulatory and institutional characteristics, and can degenerate into excess risk. This excess risk increases bank's default probability.

In this chapter we applied a two-step logit model to study the impact of the regulatory and institutional environment on excess risk, and the relationship between this factor and bank default. Applying our methodology to a micro and macro economic database (balance sheet data from Bankscope, and regulatory and institutional data from Barth *et al.* (2001) and La Porta *et al.* (1997, 1998)) of EME banks, we find evidence which validate our hypothesis.

This type of environment has a significant impact on excess risk, particularly bank regulation, regulatory discipline and the quality of the rule of law. The estimation of an excess risk indicator depending on these environmental factors allow, after controlling for capitalization, earnings and liquidity factors, better explanation and discrimination of a 1-year horizon default probability with higher default reclassification rates comparing to an alternative specification with a CAMEL binary logit model. This result holds even when we introduce these same environmental factors into CAMEL binary logit models.

The integration of an excess risk indicator, which is a function of the regulatory and institutional environment, increases the explanatory and discriminatory power of an EME bank default prediction model. Our approach proves also the importance and relevance of regulatory and institutional factors in driving excessive risk-taking behaviour.

Appendix

Table 3A.1 CAMEL – an exposition of risk factors

C	Capital adequacy measures capital buffer against unexpected losses
A	Asset quality (particularly loans portfolio quality)
M	Management quality
E	Earnings measures historical stability and composition of earnings
L	Liquidity measures bank's exposition to liquidity risk

Table 3A.2 Bank default frequency by country

Country	Country code	Available banks	Default banks	Default rate (%)
Argentina	AR	135	28	20.74
Bosnia-Herzegovina	BA	22	1	4.55
Bulgaria	BG	28	2	7.14
Bolivia	BO	16	7	43.75
Brazil	BR	188	19	10.11
Colombia	CO	56	9	16.07
Costa Rica	CR	35	3	8.57
Czech Republic	CZ	32	2	6.25
Ecuador	EC	43	2	4.65
Estonia	EE	12	4	33.33
Hong Kong	HK	105	1	0.95
Croatia	HR	48	8	16.67
Indonesia	ID	93	34	36.56
Korea (South)	KR	55	33	60.00
Lithuania	LT	13	2	15.38
Latvia	LV	28	4	14.29
Mexico	MX	46	4	8.70
Malaysia	MY	65	32	49.23
Nicaragua	NI	12	6	50.00
Panama	PA	86	8	9.30
Peru	PE	34	5	14.71
Poland	PL	58	1	1.72
Paraguay	PY	45	3	6.67
Romania	RO	36	2	5.56
Russia	RU	166	6	3.61
Singapore	SG	59	7	11.86
Slovenia	SI	27	1	3.70
Slovakia	SK	27	4	14.81
Thailand	TH	40	17	42.50
Taiwan	TW	48	3	6.25
Ukraine	UA	44	2	4.55
Uruguay	UY	57	6	10.53
Venezuela	VE	71	1	1.41
Yugoslavia	YU	23	4	17.39

Defaults are cumulated over 6 years.

Table 3A.3 Estimation results of alternative binary logit default models

Variables	CAMEL 1	CAMEL 2
NIM	−0.123**	−0.154**
	(0.05)	(0.07)
LIQATA	−0.0951***	−0.087***
	(0.02)	(0.02)
PHOLDEM	−0.982***	−1.176***
	(0.33)	(0.36)
MCAR	0.096	0.003
	(0.1)	(0.17)
DEPOSITINS	−1.562***	
	(0.43)	
FREQEXAM	−0.433	−0.249
	(0.71)	(0.89)
MISCMGTREP	1.863***	2.09***
	(0.5)	(0.53)
LEGALACT	−0.373	
	(0.5)	
PROHIBABL	2.25***	1.535***
	(0.58)	(0.55)
RULEOFLAW		0.013
		(0.24)
LEGSYSFR		−1.529*
		(0.89)
N. def.	56	49
N	727	704
χ^2	703.64***	718.08***
Log *L*	−152.1	−128.94
McFadden R^2	69.82%	73.58%
Def. reclas. rate	82.10%	81.60%

Not significant CAMEL risk factors proxies not shown.
N: number of observations; *N*. def.: number of defaults; Log *L*: logarithm of the likelihood; Def. reclas. rate: defaults correct reclassification rate. ***, ** and * significant at 1%, 5% and 10% level, respectively.

Notes

I am grateful to Michel Dietsch and Joel Petey for helpful remarks and suggestions. I thank Guillaume Horny for judicious econometric advices. I also wish to thank the participants of the Augustin Cournot Doctoral School Journey, and of the LaRGE Seminar, June 2003. I also thank the organizers and the participants of the CFS Summer School 2003, Financial Economics and Financial

Econometrics, in Eltville, Germany, the XIIIe Journées of SESAME 2003, GEMMA, Université de Caen Basse Normandie, SIFF 2003, GERME, Université de Lille 2 and the International Conference on Emerging Markets and Global Risk Management 2004, University of Westminster, London, UK. Finally, I wish to thank the regulatory institutions from the emerging market economies for their cooperation. The usual disclaimer applies.

1. For example, the banking crisis in Indonesia (1997) and Thailand (1997–98) cost about 50–55 per cent and 42.3 per cent of the GDP respectively in term of restructuring (fiscal contribution).
2. Notice that banking industry has two main specificities concerning corporate governance (see Prowse, 1995; Caprio and Levine, 2002; Ciancanelli and Gonzalez, 2000), which are: the opacity of bank assets which exacerbates the information asymmetry between insiders and outsiders, and therefore increases agency costs problem, and the regulation of the banking industry, which alters market discipline.
3. Houston and James (1995) find a positive relationship between insider's capital shares and bank charter value, which loss limits excess risk (charter value can be defined as an intangible asset which corresponds to expected future profits resulting from banking activity. It is often assimilated to the banking licence). Ang *et al.* (2001) and John *et al.* (2001) also find that this type of wage policy reduces excessive risk-taking incentives.
4. When the traditional banking activities are declining as a consequence of financial innovation and market deregulation, banks are loosing their intermediation advantage (decline of banking) (see Kaufman and More, 1994; Edwards and Mishkin, 1995; Schmidt *et al.*, 1999). In order to keep their activity profitable, banks began either to finance new activities (off-balance sheet, derivatives), or to finance riskier activities, generating excess risk (Santomero and Trester, 1998).
5. The regulation of the banking industry is mainly motivated by the negative effect of the externalities of potential bank failures (Berger *et al.*, 1995; Santos, 2001).
6. For example, failures of National Bank of San Diego or Franklin National Bank of New York in the United States.
7. These indicators reflect discipline, transparency, independence, accountability and responsibility. They are the result of interviews with bankers.
8. Protection of minority shareholders from expropriation by managers – insiders and majority shareholders.
9. Reference models are from the United States of America: SEER and SCOR models for example.
10. Since January 1997, a sixth factor has been added – *S* – for the bank's sensibility to market risk.
11. See Table 3A.1 for a brief summary of the five risk factors.
12. The evaluation of efficiency using production frontier methods permit to calculate efficiency scores. These scores measure the distance between each observation and the efficient frontier. Observations which lie on this frontier are considered as efficient (Färe *et al.*, 1994; Coelli *et al.*, 1999).

13. More efficient banks monitor their expenses, manage their risks, and anticipate the evolution of the economic environment better, in order to adapt their strategy.
14. These are information (monitoring costs), legal, political (agency costs), financial and administrative constraints.
15. She introduces a third equation which models bank's net value of the deposits insurance contribution.
16. We explain bank default probability with a 1-year time horizon.
17. With

$$p(\text{CNPL}) = \frac{e^z}{1 + e^z} \quad \text{with } z = \gamma + x_i'\varphi + \xi_i$$

$$p(\text{DEFAULT}) = \frac{e^w}{1 + e^w} \quad \text{with } w = \alpha + y_i'\beta + \varepsilon_i$$

    See Maddala (1983) and Thomas (2000) for a description and discussion of logit models.
18. Central banks, prudential regulatory and supervisory commissions, deposits insurance funds, banking associations and federations, regulatory commissions associations, and restructuring agencies.
19. NPL buyout, recapitalization.
20. Frequencies of default and available banks are shown in Table 3A.2.
21. The difference in the number of observations comes from a higher number of missing observations when we include La Porta *et al.* (1997, 1998) variables.
22. Selected CAMEL proxy ratios come from a previous study whose objective was to build an EWS type model for EME banks, which allowed us to validate the applicability of the CAMEL typology to these banks as in Godlewski (2004). We have also run two other binary logit regressions with significant variables from the CAMEL model and environmental variables used to explain the excess risk indicator in Equation 3.1 for comparison. The results are shown in Table 3A.3.
23. We only present the results of the logistic regression made on the sample corresponding to regression (3.2.1).
24. A potential positive impact of such regulation, and therefore a negative sign, concerns the restriction of bank activities to local credit markets, on which local banks have better information and can better assess its riskiness.
25. At the default rate of our sample, approximately 7 per cent.

References

Allen, F. and D. Gale (2000), *Comparing Financial Systems,* MIT Press, Cambridge, MA.

Altman, E. I., R. G. Haldeman and P. Narayanan (1977), Zeta analysis a new model to identify bankruptcy risk of corporations, *Journal of Banking and Finance* 1, 29–54.

Anderson, R. C. and D. R. Fraser (2000), Corporate control, bank risk taking and the health of the banking industry, *Journal of Banking and Finance* 24, 1383–98.

Ang, J. S., B. Lauterbach and B. Z. Schreiber (2001), Internal monitoring, regulation, and compensation of top executives in banks, *International Review of Economics and Finance* 10, 325–35.

Avery, R. B. and G. A. Hanweck (1984), A dynamic analysis of bank failures, in *Bank Structure and Competition*, pp. 380–95, Federal Reserve Bank of Chicago.

Barr, R. S. and T. F. Siems (1994), Predicting bank failure using dea to quantify management quality, *Financial Industry Studies Working Paper* 94-1, Federal Reserve Bank of Dallas.

Barr, R. S., L. M. Seiford and T. F. Siems (1993), An envelopment analysis approach to measuring the management quality of banks, *Annals of Operations Research* 45, 1–19.

Barth, J. R., G. Caprio and R. Levine (2000), Banking systems around the globe: Do regulation and ownership affect performance and stability? *Working Paper* 2325, World Bank.

Barth, J. R., G. Caprio and R. Levine (2001), The regulation and supervision of banks around the world: A new database, *Brooking-Wharton Papers on Financial Services*, ed. Litan and Herring, Washington, DC, Brookings Institution, pp. 183–250.

Barth, J. R., D. Brumbaugh, D. Sauerhaft and G. K. Wang (1985), Thrift institutions failures: Causes and policy issues, in *Bank Structure and Competition*, pp. 184–216, Federal Reserve Bank of Chicago.

Barth, J. R., D. E. Nolle, T. Phumiwasana and G. Yago (2002), A cross-country analysis of the bank supervisory framework and bank performance, *Economic and Policy Analysis Working Paper* 2, Office of the Comptroller of the Currency.

Bell, J. and D. Pain (2000), Leading indicator models of banking crises a critical review, *Financial Stability Review* 12, Bank of England.

Benston, G. J. (1985), *An Analysis of the Causes of Savings and Loan Associations Failures*, New York University monograph series in Finance and Economics edn.

Berger, A. N., R. J. Herring and G. P. Szegö (1995), The role of capital in financial institutions, *Journal of Banking and Finance* 19, 393–430.

Blum, J. (1999), Do capital adequacy requirements reduce risks in banking? *Journal of Banking and Finance* 23, 755–71.

Calomiris, C. W. and A. Powell (2000), Can emerging market bank regulators establish credible discipline? The case of Argentina, 1992–1999, *Working Paper* 7715, NBER.

Caprio, G. and D. Klingebiel (1996), Bank insolvencies: Cross country experience, *Working Paper* 1620, World Bank.

Caprio, G. and R. Levine (2002), Corporate governance in finance: Concepts and international observations, in *Building the Pillars of Financial Sector Governance: The Roles of the Private and Public Sectors*, The Brookings Institution Press.

Ciancanelli, P. and J. A. Reyes Gonzalez (2000), Corporate governance in banking: A conceptual framework, *Working Paper*.
Clair, R. T. (1992), Loan growth and loan quality: Some preliminary evidence from Texas banks, *Economic Review*, Federal Reserve Bank of Dallas.
Coelli, T., D. S. Prasada Rao and G. E. Battese (1999), *An Introduction to Efficiency and Productivity Analysis*, Kluwer Academic Publishers, Dordrecht.
Cordella, T. and E. Levy Yeyati (2002), Financial opening, deposit insurance, and risk in a model of banking competition, *European Economic Review* 46, 471–85.
Covitz, D. and E. Heitfield (1999), Monitoring, moral hazard, and market power: A model of bank lending, *Finance and Economics Discussion Series* 37, Federal Reserve Board.
Demirgüç-Kunt, A. (1989a), Deposit-institution failures: A review of empirical literature, *Economic Review* 25, Federal Reserve Bank of Cleveland.
Demirgüç-Kunt, A. (1989b), Modelling large commercial bank failures: A simultaneous-equation analysis, *Working Paper* 8905, Federal Reserve Bank of Cleveland.
Demirgüç-Kunt, A. and E. Detragiarche (2000), Monitoring banking sector fragility: A multivariate logit approach, *World Bank Economic Review* 14, 287–307.
Demsetz, R. S., M. R. Saidenberg and P. E. Strahan (1997), Agency problems and risk taking, *Staff Reports* 29, Federal Reserve Bank of New York.
Edwards, F. R. and F. S. Mishkin (1995), The decline of traditional banking: Implications for financial stability and regulatory policy, *Economic Policy Review*, Federal Reserve Bank of New York.
Färe, R., S. Grosskopf and C. A. K. Lovell (1994), *Production Frontiers*, Cambridge University Press, Cambridge.
Gajewski, G. R. (1988), Bank risk, regulator behaviour, and bank closure in the mid 1980's: A two step logit model, PhD Dissertation, George Washington University.
Godlewski, C. J. (2004), Modélisation de la prévision de la défaillance bancaire: Une application aux banques des pays emergents, *Working Paper* 70, LaRGE, Université Robert Schuman.
Goldstein, M. and P. Turner (1996), Banking crises in emerging economies: Origins and policy options, *BIS Economic Papers* 46, Bank for International Settlements.
Gonzalez-Hermosillo, B. (1999), Determinants of ex-ante banking system distress: A macro-micro empirical exploration of some recent episodes, *Working Paper* 33, International Monetary Fund.
Gorton, G. and R. Rosen (1995), Corporate control, portfolio choice and the decline of banking, *Journal of Finance* 50, 1377–420.
Hellmann, T. F., K. C. Murdock and J. E. Stiglitz (2000), Liberalization, moral hazard in banking, and prudential regulation: Are capital requirements enough? *American Economic Review* 90, 147–65.
Honohan, P. (1997), Banking system failures in developing and transition countries: Diagnosis and predictions, *Working Paper* 39, Bank for International Settlements.

Houston, J. F. and C. James (1995), CEO compensation and bank risk; is compensation in banking structured to promote risk taking? *Journal of Monetary Economics* 36, 405–31.

Hussain, Q. and C. Wihlborg (1999), Corporate insolvency procedures and bank behaviour: A study of selected Asian economies, *Working Paper* 135, International Monetary Fund.

Jensen, M. C. (1993), Presidential address: The modern industrial revolution, exit and failure of internal control systems, *Journal of Finance* 48, 831–80.

John, K., A. Saunders and L. W. Senbet (2001), A theory of bank regulation and management compensation, *Review of Financial Studies* 13, 95–125.

Kane, E. J. (1989), *The S&L Insurance Mess: How Did It Happen?* The Urban Institute, Washington, DC.

Kaufman, G. G. and L. R. More (1994), Is banking a declining industry? A historical perspective, *Economic Perspectives*, Federal Reserve Bank of Chicago.

Keeley, M. C. (1990), Deposit insurance, risk, and market power in banking, *American Economic Review* 80, 1183–200.

Keeton, W. R. and C. S. Morris (1987), Why do banks' loan losses differ? *Economic Review* 72, Federal Reserve Bank of Kansas City.

Kim, D. and A. M. Santomero (1988), Risk in banking and capital regulation, *Journal of Finance* 43, 1219–33.

Klapper, L. F. and I. Love (2002), Corporate governance, investor protection, and performance in emerging markets, *Policy Research Working Paper* 2818, World Bank.

Knopf, J. D. and J. L. Teall (1996), Risk taking behaviour in the US thrift industry: Ownership structure and regulatory changes, *Journal of Banking and Finance* 20, 1329–50.

Koehn, M. and A. M. Santomero (1980), Regulation of bank capital and portfolio risk, *Journal of Finance* 35, 1235–50.

La Porta, R., F. Lopez de Silanes and A. Shleifer (1998), Law and finance, *Journal of Political Economy* 106, 1113–55.

La Porta, R., F. Lopez de Silanes, A. Shleifer and R. W. Vishny (1997), Legal determinants of external finance, *Journal of Finance* 52, 1130–50.

La Porta, R., F. Lopez de Silanes, A. Shleifer and R. W. Vishny (2000), Investor protection and corporate governance, *Journal of Financial Economics* 58, 3–27.

Llellewyn, D. T. (2002), An analysis of the causes of recent banking crises, *European Journal of Finance* 8, 152–75.

Maddala, G. S. (1983), *Limited Dependent and Qualitative Variables in Econometrics*, Cambridge University Press, Cambridge.

Martin, D. (1977), Early warning of bank failure, *Journal of Banking and Finance* 1, 249–76.

Mitton, T. (2002), A cross-firm analysis of the impact of corporate governance of the east Asian financial crisis, *Journal of Financial Economics* 64, 215–41.

OCC (1988), Bank failure an evaluation of the factors contributing to the failure of national banks, *Discussion Paper*, Office of the Comptroller of the Currency.

Pantalone, C. C. and M. B. Platt (1987), Predicting commercial bank failures since deregulation, *New England Economic Review*, 37–47.

Prowse, S. D. (1995), Alternative methods of corporate control in commercial banks, *Economic Review*, Federal Reserve Bank of Dallas.
Repullo, R. (2004), Capital requirements, market power, and risk taking in banking, *Journal of Financial Intermediation* 13, 156–82.
Santomero, A. M. and J. Trester (1998), Financial innovation and bank risk taking, *Journal of Economic Behaviour and Organization* 35, 25–37.
Santos, J. A. (2001), Bank capital regulation in contemporary banking theory: A review of the literature, *Financial Markets, Institutions and Instruments* 10, 41–84.
Saunders, A. and B. K. Wilson (2001), An analysis of bank charter value and its risk constraining incentives, *Journal of Financial Services Research* 19, 185–95.
Saunders, A., S. Strock and N. G. Travlos (1990), Ownership structure, deregulation, and bank risk taking, *Journal of Finance* 45, 643–54.
Schmidt, R. H., A. Hackerthal and M. Tyrell (1999), Disintermediation and the role of banks in Europe: An international comparison, *Journal of Financial Intermediation* 8, 36–67.
Sinkey, J. F. (1975), A multivariate statistical analysis of the characteristics of problem banks, *Journal of Finance* 30, 21–36.
Thomas, A. (2000), *Econométrie des Variables Qualitatives*, Dunod.
Thomson, J. B. (1992), Modelling the bank regulator's closure option: A two step logit regression approach, *Journal of Financial Services Research* 6, 5–23.

4
Modelling Long Memory and Risk Premia in Latin American Sovereign Bond Markets

Alfonso Mendoza V.

4.1 Introduction

Emerging bond markets (EBMs) have become one of the largest and most liquid international markets. The amount of debt outstanding is more than US$300 billion and the issuance by four countries – Argentina, Brazil, Mexico and Venezuela – accounts for 90 per cent or more of the total market debt in Latin America. These four issuers also drive around 50–60 per cent of most international emerging market bond indexes (EMBIs).

Interpreted as measures of default or credit risks, EMBIs have been associated to capital flows, market sentiment and fundamentals (GDP, stock markets, goods prices, interest rates and various other variables).[1]

This chapter analyses daily sovereign credit spreads in Latin America as proxied by the individual EMBI of JPMorgan. The main feature of this work with respect to previous studies is the suggestion that excess holding returns in these markets are driven mainly by conditional time-varying risk premia. Research into EMBIs has not yet explored the possibility of excess returns being predicted by their own conditional volatilities, which we assume fully reflect information about fundamentals.

Some studies have found some degree of predictability in EMBI but have failed to take it into account at the modeling stage.[2] We find here that spreads are in fact fractionally integrated, hence indicating a high degree of predictability in these markets. Long memory (LM) or long-range dependency has not been investigated in EBMs.

Some authors have documented already the high degree of cross correlation in this market as well as a remarkable comovement and potential common shocks in levels and volatility (see Mauro *et al.*, 2000; Jostova, 2002; Fiess, 2003). In our view, these studies have been nonetheless unsuccessful to capture the strong *fractional* long-run cross dependence in these markets.

The contribution of this chapter is twofold. First, the stationary LM properties of the volatility in these markets are investigated for the first time. In contrast with some studies suggesting that EMBIs exhibit unit roots, this study provides strong evidence of stationarity and LM. Second, we propose a new family of bivariate long memory models for credit risk that take into account risk premia, the high degree of correlation, individual persistency and co-persistency.

In econometric terms we provide the empirical literature with a new bivariate fractional integrated generalized autoregressive conditional heteroskedasticity model with in-mean terms (FIGARCH-in-mean). Quasi-maximum likelihood estimation (QMLE) results as well as the Schwartz information criterion for these markets suggest that these new models give superior estimates compared to previous bivariate FIGARCH specifications. There is indeed a significant gain of information by including the risk premium in the modelling of sovereign default spreads.

The following section provides a descriptive analysis of EMBI spreads and its autocorrelation functions. The LM and stationarity properties of volatility are also investigated. Interestingly, a battery of both heuristic and semiparametric methods confirm the existence of LM stationarity in volatility.

Univariate LM models and the econometric models of Teyssière (1997) and Brunetti and Christopher (2000) are described in detail in Section 3. These models are extended to the new bivariate FIGARCH (1,d,1)-in-mean specification. QMLE results are reported in Section 4. Policy implications and the significance of our findings to the understanding of Sovereign EBMs are discussed in the conclusions.

4.2 Descriptive analysis and long-run dependence

4.2.1 Descriptive analysis of default spreads in EBM

Figure 4.1 shows the EMBI spreads[3] in levels for Brazil, Mexico and Venezuela from 31 December 1990 to 10 July 2002. The Argentinean

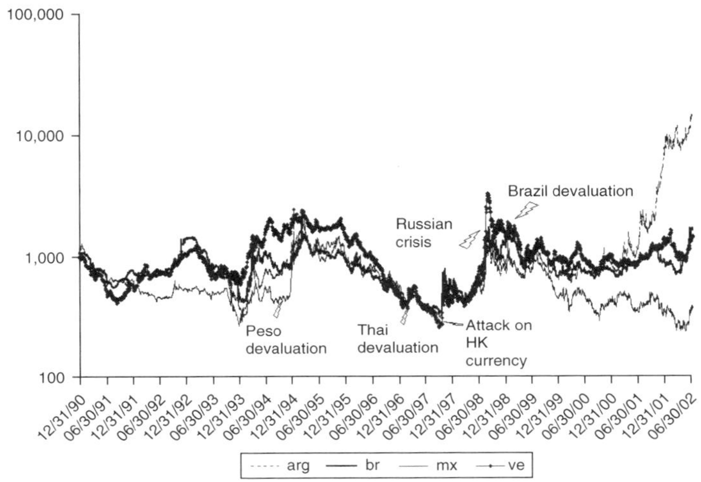

Figure 4.1 EMBI spreads, 31 December 1990–30 June 2002

sample begins on 30 April 1993. EMBI spreads, or S_t, provide a single measure of pure sovereign default risk and may be readily interpreted as excess returns over US treasuries.[4] A relatively high spread may indicate a greater risk of default[5] and also a lower return on risk-free investments. EMBI spreads are also commonly regarded as the premium for holding defaultable sovereign instruments.

A salient feature of these markets is the high degree of comovement. Some authors have already documented a high degree of interdependence between EMBI spreads, common trends and common shocks (see, e.g., Mauro *et al.*, 2000; Fiess, 2003). In addition, the data suggests that risk premia are time varying and also that the relative spread difference between two given countries is not stable.[6] For all these reasons, the kinetics of EMBI should be analyzed in a multivariate setting rather than on an individual basis.

The first differences of the spreads in logs, that are named here as s_t are presented in Figure 4.2. By definition, spread changes can be interpreted as changes in *excess returns* over US treasuries. These reflect general emerging market (EM) prospects and hence the credit risk[7] attached to EM assets (see Cunninham *et al.*, 2001).

It is interesting to observe that individual spread changes seem to exhibit a common response to shocks. For instance, periods of distress

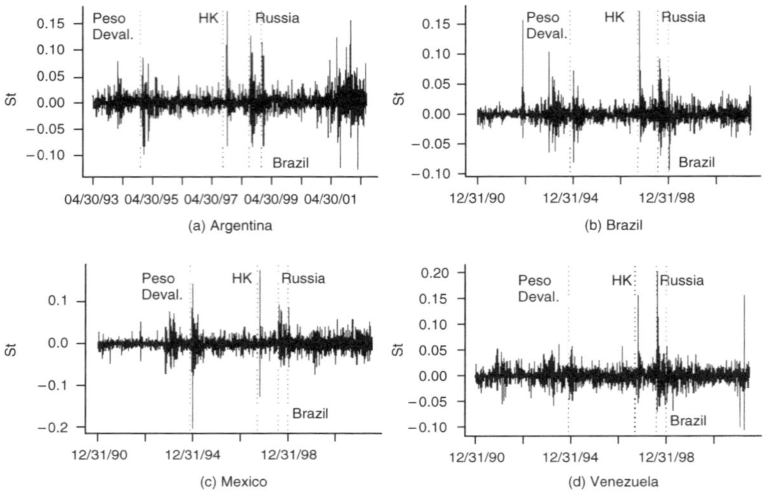

Figure 4.2 EMBI spread changes to 10 July 2002

such as the Tequila Crisis in December 1994 not only affected the Mexican default risk and volatility, but also affected other Latin American bond indexes. What is more, these markets also seem to respond very rapidly to turmoils generated in other latitudes, for example, Hong Kong or Russia. The common response to shocks in levels and volatility implies that there may be a common factor driving these markets in the same direction.[8]

Figure 4.2 also shows that individual credit risks share some of the stylized facts of financial returns such as the presence of clusters and some degree of time dependence. There is no reason to rule out a priori the potential for high comovement and time varying volatility. Summary descriptive statistics are presented in Table 4.1. The series show a similar risk–return relationship, the returns exhibit high kurtosis and there is indeed evidence of time series dependence as indicated by the twentieth-order Ljung–Box statistic.

4.2.2 Long memory in EBMs

To examine the autocorrelation pattern further, Figure 4.3 graphically analyses the dependence structure of individual EBM spreads. The autocorrelation functions (ACF) of spread changes (s_t) and of its absolute

Table 4.1 EMBI, descriptive statistics, daily spread changes (s_t) in logs

s_t[a]	$\bar{x}$	σ	S[b]	K[c]	JB[d]	Min.	Max.	n	LB(20)[e]
Argentina	0.0005	0.0188	0.8775	11.61	13,780	−0.1274	0.1709	2,398	67.61*
Brazil	0.0001	0.0130	1.9415	24.60	77,712	−0.0934	0.1725	3,007	96.25*
Mexico	−0.0002	0.0164	0.3330	18.95	45,041	−0.2031	0.1764	3,007	82.05*
Venezuela	0.0001	0.0147	1.7089	24.60	77,299	−0.1045	0.2020	3,007	101.69*

* Significant at the 1% level.
[a] $s_t = \log(S_t) - \log(S_{t-1})$ where S_t is the EMBI spread.
[b] Skewness.
[c] Kurtosis.
[d] Jarque–Bera statistic.
[e] Ljung–Box statistic, order in brackets.

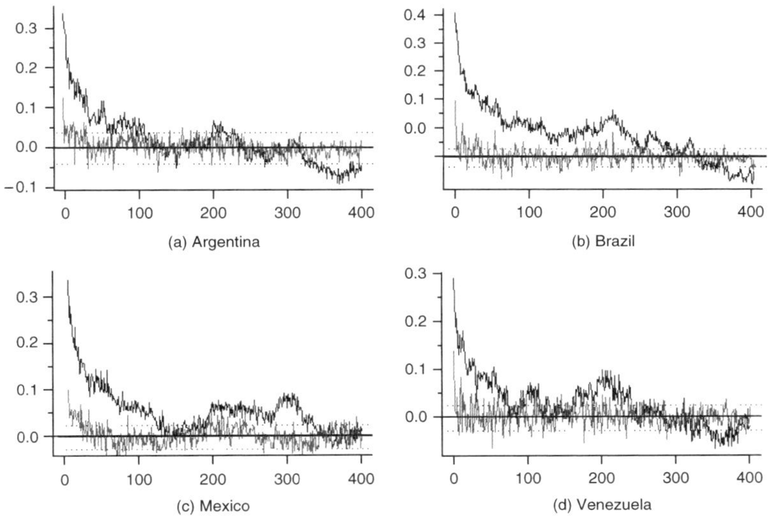

Figure 4.3 Autocorrelation of $|s_t|$ and s_t from high to low: EMBI daily log difference, 31 December 1990–10 July 2002

transformation ($|s_t|$) are bounded by a 95 per cent confidence interval.[9] It is observed, with no exception, that the ACF associated with s_t presents an exponential decay rate – see lighter lines – that is, significant autocorrelations are reported only for the first lags, while the rate of convergence of the ACF for $|s_t|$ is much slower (see dark lines). Most of the countries present significant absolute value autocorrelations for more than one hundred lags while Brazil, panel (b), has the first negative autocorrelation not earlier than lag 350. This is fully consistent with Ding and Granger (1996) who have suggested that a time series shows LM if the rate of decay of the estimated conditional variances seems hyperbolic rather than exponential.

LM is also present in combinations of bond spreads. To illustrate, Figure 4.4 shows the linear cross correlation of a portfolio consisting of two assets: Brazil and Mexico. The ACF of simple spread changes is denoted by $\rho_{mx,br}$ in grey lines, while absolute transforms, that is, $\rho_{|mx,br|}$, are shown in dark lines. Panels (a) and (b) show the ACF up to lag 400, while panels (c) and (d) show a 60-day zoom of the cross correlations.

As with individual ACF, cross correlograms in Figure 4.4 suggest that simple cross correlations decay exponentially, while the ACF of absolute transforms exhibit a hypergeometric decay rate. The graphical examination suggests strong and significant long-run volatility cross dependencies in the absolute values of spread changes (see dark lines in panels (a) and (b)).

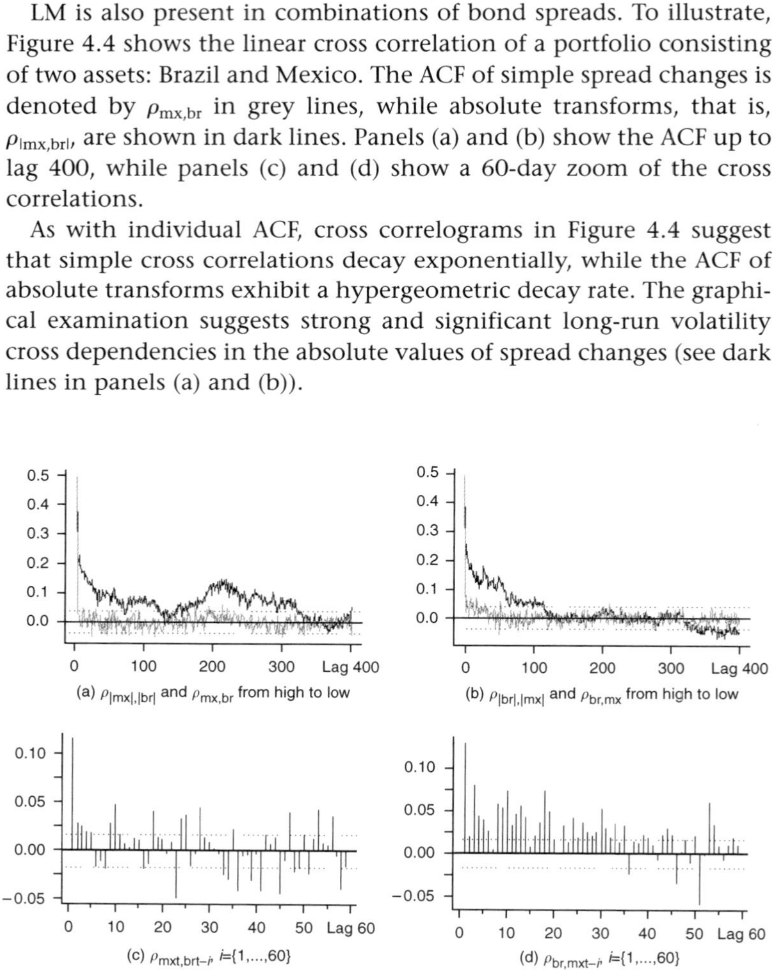

Figure 4.4 Cross correlogram EMBI Mexico versus Brazil for $|s_t|$ and s_t

Table 4.2 EMBI, cross correlations at different lag values

lag(i)	1	10	50	100	150	200	300	Neg.[a]	Spill[b]
Panel (a): $\rho_{1t,2t-i}$									
$\rho_{art,brt-i}$	0.5864	0.1087	0.0232	0.0074	−0.0145	0.0526	−0.0077	65	55
$\rho_{art,mxt-i}$	0.5041	0.1341	0.0544	0.0000	−0.0441	−0.0013	0.0198	67	59
$\rho_{art,vet-i}$	0.4340	0.0688	0.0165	−0.0064	−0.0648	−0.0119	−0.0065	47	40
$\rho_{brt,mxt-i}$	0.4917	0.1702	0.1411	0.0559	0.0214	0.0265	0.0015	124	116
$\rho_{brt,vet-i}$	0.4862	0.1416	0.1218	0.0652	0.0516	0.0442	0.0118	158	151
$\rho_{mxt,vet-i}$	0.4204	0.1233	0.0669	0.0596	0.0242	0.0565	0.0638	139	130
Panel (b): $\rho_{2t,1t-i}$									
$\rho_{brt,art-i}$	0.5864	0.0958	0.0412	0.0068	−0.0062	0.0015	0.0030	63	57
$\rho_{mxt,art-i}$	0.5041	0.1254	0.0469	0.0243	−0.0077	0.0125	0.0259	66	58
$\rho_{vet,art-i}$	0.4340	0.0579	0.0158	0.0193	−0.0009	0.0613	−0.0180	36	30
$\rho_{mxt,brt-i}$	0.4917	0.1734	0.0580	0.0679	0.0590	0.1319	0.0696	128	120
$\rho_{vet,brt-i}$	0.4862	0.1395	0.0840	0.0823	0.0613	0.1378	−0.0009	290	286
$\rho_{vet,mxt-i}$	0.4204	0.1157	0.0632	0.0424	0.0027	0.0549	−0.0105	80	70

Note: The confidence interval is approximated using ±two standard errors. For portfolios containing Argentinean bonds this equals 0.0417 and for all other portfolios it is 0.0365.
[a] Lag at which the first negative value is observed.
[b] Lag at which the autocorrelation function first crosses the horizontal axis.

In Table 4.2 we present a summary of the cross long-range dependence properties for the series under analysis. The first column shows the lead/lag relationships of the six portfolios as represented by the cross correlation coefficients $\rho_{it,jt-i}$ and $\rho_{jt,jt-i}$. There is an equal contemporaneous response between countries only for the first lags and apparent asymmetric impacts afterwards (see first column of panels (a) and (b)). Except for the pair Argentina Mexico, all countries show significant cross correlations at least until lag 50.

In the last column of Table 4.2 we show the point at which the last significant positive correlation takes place and label it as 'spillover'. This measure indicates the dependence of contemporaneous spreads with lagged values. As we observe in panels (a) and (b) the volatility dependence structure is in general highly symmetric: volatility shocks disseminate at similar rates from one country to another.

Overall, this section has shown evidence of LM in the credit risk series of EBM. The high persistency may be explained, in agreement with Jostova (2002), as the result of financial market rigidities and informational deficiencies. Portfolio re-allocation after a sudden liquidity crunch for instance may not be immediate due to the way institutional investors operate in EBMs[10] and the lack of 'noise traders' among other factors. Also, dedicated investors may react more slowly to market signals since they pursue returns relative to a benchmark.

The rigorous reader may note that an LM diagnosis based on the graphical inspection of autocorrelation and cross-correlation functions may be spurious. It can be argued reasonably that LM may in fact be nothing other than the result of structural changes in the data and monotonic trends (see Lobato and Robinson, 1998; Giraitis *et al.*, 2002). To rule out this possibility, we have formally tested for the presence of LM on (s_t), on spread volatility proxies ($|s_t|$ and $|s_t|^d$) and on nonlinear transforms ($|s_{it}s_{jt}|$) using semiparametric methods. The results, not presented here to save space, are qualitatively similar and reassuringly confirm the presence of LM in EBMs.[11]

4.3 Parametric LM in volatility

We have shown in the previous section that the volatility of credit risks in EBMs exhibits LM. To model this property we need a process that is not only able to capture individual long-run dependence, but also allows us to take into account fractional comovement, the response to common shocks and also provides estimates of risk premia. The aim of this section is to introduce and develop such a family of credit risk models.

4.3.1 Univariate FIGARCH

Arguably the most popular parametric process that replicates the strong dependence in volatility, that is, hypergeometric decay of the ACF, is the FIGARCH model of Bollerslev and Mikkelsen (1996).[12]

To begin with, let us assume for simplicity that excess returns in EBMs for each individual case follow a random walk process plus drift (c):

$$s_t = c + \varepsilon_t \tag{4.1}$$

To capture the time varying conditional volatility of the residuals ε_t it may be proposed that:

$$\varepsilon_t|\Omega_{t-1} = \eta_t\sqrt{h_t} \tag{4.2}$$

where η_t is an independent identically distributed (i.i.d.) random process with mean equal to zero and variance equal to unity. Notice that $E(\varepsilon_t|\Omega_{t-1}) = 0$ and $\text{Var}(\varepsilon_t|\Omega_{t-1}) = h_t$.

Baillie *et al.* (1996) have proposed the following FIGARCH process for h_t:

$$\varepsilon_t^2(1 - \phi)(1 - L)^d = w + (1 - \beta L)\upsilon_t \tag{4.3}$$

where L is the lag operator, $\phi = (\alpha + \beta)$ the mean reverting parameter, $\upsilon_t = \varepsilon_t^2 - h_t$, $(1 - L)$ is the first differencing operator and d is the fractional integration parameter.

This model reduces to the parsimonious GARCH(1,1) process of Bollerslev (1986) when $d = 0$ and to the IGARCH(1,1) process of Engle and Bollerslev (1986) when $d = 1$. In the first case, shocks to the conditional variance decay at an exponential rate; while in the second, shocks remain important for forecasts of all horizons. In a FIGARCH process with $0 < d < 1$, shocks to the variance decay at a hyperbolic rate replicating well the graphical behaviour observed in the second section of this chapter.

The fractional differencing operator has a binomial expansion that can be conveniently expressed in terms of the Gamma function:

$$\begin{aligned}(1 - L)^d &= F(-d,1,1;L)\\ &= \sum_{k=0}^{\infty}\Gamma(k - d)\Gamma(k + 1)^{-1}\Gamma(-d)^{-1}L^k\\ &= \sum_{k=0}^{\infty}\pi_k L^k\end{aligned} \tag{4.4}$$

The infinite ARCH representation of this FIGARCH(1,d,1) process, is obtained by rearranging Equation 4.3:

$$\begin{aligned}h_t &= \frac{\omega}{1 - \beta(1)} + \left[1 - \frac{(1 - \phi L)(1 - L)^d}{1 - \beta L}\right]\varepsilon_t^2\\ h_t &= \frac{\omega}{1 - \beta(1)} + \lambda(L)\varepsilon_t^2\end{aligned} \tag{4.5}$$

where $\lambda(L) = \lambda_1 L + \lambda_2 L + \cdots$. To ensure positiveness of the conditional variance all the coefficients in the infinite ARCH representation must be nonnegative. In particular, for the case of the FIGARCH (1,d,1) process in Equation 4.5 the conditions for the process to be well defined and positive have been given by Baillie *et al.* (1996) and

Bollerslev and Mikkelsen (1996). These can be observed if we re-express the lag polynomial $\lambda(L)$ in Equation 4.5 as:

$$\begin{aligned} \lambda_1 &= \phi - \beta + d \\ \lambda_k &= \beta\lambda_{k-1} + [(k-1-d)k^{-1} - \phi]\delta_{k-1} \quad \text{for } k \geq 2 \\ \delta_k &= \delta_{k-1}(k-1-d)k^{-1}, \quad k = 2,3, \ldots \end{aligned} \tag{4.6}$$

where δ_k are the coefficients in the Maclaurin's series expansion. From here, Bollerslev and Mikkelsen (1996) show sufficient conditions under which all corresponding ARCH parameters are non-negative:

$$\begin{aligned} &\beta - d \leq \phi \leq (2-d)/3 \\ &d[\phi - (1-d)/2] \leq \beta(\phi - \beta + d) \end{aligned} \tag{4.7}$$

Baillie *et al.* (1996) explain that for $0 < d \leq 1$ the Gamma function evaluated at $L = 1$ equals 0 so that $\lambda(1) = 1$. For this reason the second moment of the unconditional distribution of λ_t is infinite and the FIGARCH process is clearly not weakly stationary. However, by extending the properties of IGARCH processes, Nelson (1991) and Bougerol and Picard (1992) show that the FIGARCH process is still strictly stationary and ergodic.

4.3.2 Bivariate fractional GARCH

The cross-correlation coefficient has become the widely preferred statistic to examine the comovement of sovereign spreads since this measure provides information on the speed, degree and direction of contagion.[13] Even though this seems a very convenient measure for short-term cross market dependencies, this indicator is subject to at least three major criticisms: it does not take into account the fractional comovement of these markets, it does not consider the time varying volatility[14] and it disregards the existence of risk premia.

Based on the flexibility of Bollerslev (1990) constant correlation coefficient model (CCC), it is possible to use the correlation coefficient as a measure of interdependence while simultaneously taking into account the individual behaviour of volatilities. Such parametrization assumes that the correlation matrix of the vector of residuals is constant – a very strong assumption in EBMs – but at the same time allows the individual volatilities contained in the conditional *variance-covariance* matrix (H_t) to be time varying. In addition, by employing Brunetti and Christopher (2000) bivariate specification,[15] the individual conditional variances $h_{1,t}$, $h_{2,t}$ are assumed to take FIGARCH processes as follows:

$$\boldsymbol{\varepsilon}_t|_{t-1} \sim N(0,H_t), \quad \{H_t\} = h_{ij,t} \tag{4.8}$$

$$\begin{aligned} h_{ii,t} &= \frac{\omega_i}{1-\beta_{ii}(1)} + \lambda_{ii}(L)\varepsilon_{i,t}^2 \quad \text{for } i = 1,2 \\ h_{12,t} &= \rho_{12}\sqrt{h_{11},_t}\sqrt{h_{22},_t} \end{aligned} \tag{4.9}$$

where

$$\lambda_{ii}(L) = \left[1 - \frac{(1-\phi_{ii}L)(1-L)^{di}}{1-\beta_{ii}L}\right] \quad \text{for } i = 1,2 \text{ and } \boldsymbol{\varepsilon}_t = [\varepsilon_1,\varepsilon_2].$$

In order for H_t to be positive definite it is required that $h_{11,t}$ and $h_{22,t}$ are positive and the conditional correlation matrix is positive definite. Bollerslev (1990) noticed that under the assumption of time invariant correlations, the maximum likelihood estimate (MLE) of the correlation matrix is equal to the sample correlation matrix of the standardized residuals. Hence, this is a parsimonious specification where positive definiteness of the variance-covariance matrix is ensured provided that $|\rho| < 1$, $\beta_{ii} - d_i \leq (1/3)(2 - d_i)$ and $d_i[\phi_{ii} - 1/2 \cdot (1 - d_i)] \leq [\beta_{ii}(\phi_{ii} - \beta_{ii} + d_i)]$. Also the conditional variance of the system is stationarity for all $0 \leq d_i \leq 1$ (see Brunetti and Christopher, 2000).

Analogous to the individual representation in Equation 4.3, Brunetti and Christopher (2000) present the CCC–FARIMA representation in terms of the squared residuals as

$$\Phi(L)\begin{pmatrix}(1-L)^{d_1} & 0 \\ 0 & (1-L)^{d_2}\end{pmatrix}\begin{pmatrix}\varepsilon_{1t}^2 \\ \varepsilon_{2t}^2\end{pmatrix} = w + B(L)\nu_t \tag{4.10}$$

where $\Phi(L) = B_0 = I$. From this form, it is clear that a direct testing for common orders of LM, that is, $d_1 = d_2$, is possible.

A constant correlation assumption may be far too restrictive given the episodes of distress in EBMs during the nineties. More importantly perhaps, none of the parameters in Equation 4.10 captures the time varying interdependence evident in the descriptive section before.

In order to explore the possibility of time varying correlation, Teyssière (1997) relaxed the constancy assumption by allowing the conditional *covariance* to be represented by a FIGARCH process too. Assuming a random walk plus drift for the mean we get:

$$
\begin{aligned}
s_{it} &= c_i + \varepsilon_{it} \\
s_{jt} &= c_j + \varepsilon_{jt} \\
h_{ij} &= w_{ij} + \left(1 - \frac{(1 - \phi_{ij} L)(1 - L)^{d_{ij}}}{1 - \beta_{ij} L}\right)\varepsilon_{it-k}\,\varepsilon_{jt-k}, \quad i,j = 1,2
\end{aligned}
\tag{4.11}
$$

This innovative extension allows to capture and test the presence of long-range cross dependencies. In particular the parameter d_{ij} becomes a natural measure of volatility contagion and fractional comovement. It also captures the effect of volatilities and is fully consistent with the perception of Forbes and Rigobon (1999) who argue that contagion is not the result of changing autocorrelations but derives from changing volatilities.

As pointed out by Teyssière (1997) there is no analytical set of conditions for ensuring positive definiteness of the conditional variance–covariance so this has to be implemented numerically in the estimation algorithm.

4.3.3 Bivariate fractional GARCH-in-mean process

Our new model proposals are introduced here and in the following sections. As before, it is assumed that credit risks follow a random walk plus drift. The key contribution to the existing bivariate FIGARCH models is the inclusion of risk premia as regressors of spread changes:

$$
\begin{aligned}
s_{1t} &= c_1 + \gamma_{11}h_{1t} + \gamma_{12}h_{2t} + \varepsilon_{1t} \\
s_{2t} &= c_2 + \gamma_{21}h_{1t} + \gamma_{22}h_{2t} + \varepsilon_{2t} \\
h_{1t} &= \frac{w_1}{1 - \beta_{11}L} + \left(1 - \frac{(1 - \phi_{11}L)(1 - L)^{d_1}}{1 - \beta_{11}L}\right)\varepsilon_{1,t}^2 \\
h_{2t} &= \frac{w_2}{1 - \beta_{22}L} + \left(1 - \frac{(1 - \phi_{22}L)(1 - L)^{d_2}}{1 - \beta_{22}L}\right)\varepsilon_{2,t}^2 \\
h_{12} &= \rho_{1,2}\sqrt{h_{11,t}}\sqrt{h_{22,t}}
\end{aligned}
\tag{4.12}
$$

As an additional feature, in the empirical section we will not only employ the cross-conditional variances (h_{1t} or h_{2t}) in Equation 4.12 as regressors but also the conditional covariances, that is, h_{12t}, in order to capture the association between spread changes and fundamentals as in Baillie and Bollerslev (1990).

Notice also that similar to Teyssière (1997) this model can easily be extended by relaxing the assumption of time invariant correlation, in which case we would have an extra equation in the variance process describing the dynamics of the conditional covariances and hence an estimate of the fractional comovement parameter (d_{12}) as follows:

$$\begin{aligned}
s_{1t} &= c_1 + \gamma_{11}h_{1t} + \gamma_{12}h_{2t} + \varepsilon_{1t} \\
s_{2t} &= c_2 + \gamma_{21}h_{1t} + \gamma_{22}h_{2t} + \varepsilon_{2t} \\
h_{1t} &= \frac{w_1}{1 - \beta_{11}L} + \left(1 - \frac{(1 - \phi_{11}L)(1 - L)^{d_1}}{1 - \beta_{11}L}\right)\varepsilon^2_{1,t} \\
h_{2t} &= \frac{w_2}{1 - \beta_{22}L} + \left(1 - \frac{(1 - \phi_{22}L)(1 - L)^{d_2}}{1 - \beta_{22}L}\right)\varepsilon^2_{2,t} \\
h_{12t} &= \frac{w_{12}}{1 - \beta_{12}L} + \left(1 - \frac{(1 - \phi_{12}L)(1 - L)^{d_{12}}}{1 - \beta_{12}L}\right)\varepsilon_{1,t}\varepsilon_{2,t}
\end{aligned} \tag{4.13}$$

Model 4.13 can also include cross conditional covariances in mean replacing individual variances. In this case, as well as the Teyssière's (1997) model, the positivity conditions have not been derived analytically and hence they have to be imposed during estimation.

Empirical findings for high frequency financial returns suggest in general that FIGARCH(1,d,1) innovations are usually non-normal and exhibit serial autocorrelation. To account for such possibility in the estimation of these models we use the QMLE approach of Bollerslev and Wooldridge (1992).[16]

4.4 Estimation results

We now present the bivariate QMLE estimations for the credit risk models introduced in the previous section. We assume that investors hold pair-based portfolios and have four Latin American bonds to choose from a total of six combinations.

4.4.1 Common LM

Decision criteria prefer random walk models for the mean and FIGARCH(1,d,1) processes for the variance equation.[17] To capture long-run comovement between sovereign markets, Table 4.3 reports the QMLE estimations of Equation 4.9,[18] the bivariate Constant Correlation long memory model.

All the estimates are highly significant. The behaviour of the individual conditional variances (h_{11} and h_{22}) is fully described by the mean reversion (ϕ and β) and persistence (d) parameters.

As expected from the graphical analysis before, all the correlation coefficients are large and positive, indicating a greater systematic risk

Table 4.3 EMBI, CCC–FIGARCH(1,d,1) QMLE estimations

	(s_{art}, s_{brt})[a]	(s_{art}, s_{mxt})	(s_{art}, s_{vet})	(s_{brt}, s_{mxt})	(s_{brt}, s_{vet})	(s_{mxt}, s_{vet})
Conditional mean						
μ_1	−0.0427	−0.0479	−0.0418	−0.0174	−0.0267	−0.0402
	(0.0227)[b]	(0.0240)	(0.0247)	(0.0128)	(0.0132)	(0.0176)
μ_2	−0.0657	−0.0577	−0.0644	−0.0270	−0.0317	−0.0332
	(0.0158)	(0.0224)	(0.0224)	(0.0169)	(0.0201)	(0.0202)
Conditional variances						
ω_1	0.1428	0.1433	0.1318	0.0327	0.0374	0.0424
	(0.0133)	(0.0143)	(0.0245)	(0.0058)	(0.0059)	(0.0069)
β_1	0.4446	0.4878	0.2817	0.5004	0.5029	0.5451
	(0.0229)	(0.0288)	(0.1019)	(0.0222)	(0.0212)	(0.0204)
φ_1	0.3162	0.2686	0.0897	0.2820	0.2886	0.3041
	(0.0178)	(0.0201)	(0.0914)	(0.0149)	(0.0147)	(0.0160)
d_1	0.3675	0.4628	0.3371	0.4361	0.4229	0.3918
	(0.0355)	(0.0402)	(0.0351)	(0.0298)	(0.0295)	(0.0319)
ω_2	0.0941	0.1363	0.1067	0.0506	0.1569	0.1433
	(0.0173)	(0.0173)	(0.0231)	(0.0076)	(0.0204)	(0.0198)
β_2	0.2234	0.6218	0.4449	0.5469	0.3995	0.3915
	(0.1196)	(0.0592)	(0.0318)	(0.0226)	(0.0243)	(0.0264)
φ_2	0.0615	0.1437	0.3509	0.2964	0.3826	0.3789
	(0.1031)	(0.0381)	(0.0200)	(0.0172)	(0.0127)	(0.0133)
d_2	0.4296	0.6693	0.2981	0.4073	0.2348	0.2422
	(0.0353)	(0.0716)	(0.0400)	(0.0343)	(0.0255)	(0.0267)
ρ_{12}	0.7155	0.6078	0.5998	0.5189	0.5624	0.4944
	(0.0052)	(0.0074)	(0.0109)	(0.0099)	(0.0109)	(0.0108)

[a] (s_{it}, s_{jt}) indicate the bond components in a given portfolio.
[b] Robust standard errors in parenthesis.

effect – that is, the risk of the portfolio that cannot be diversified away – on these portfolios. The highest correlation is observed in Argentina–Brazil with 71.6 per cent, while the correlation of Argentina with Mexico and Venezuela is 60.8 and 59.9 per cent, respectively. The correlation for the rest of the portfolios is no less than 49 per cent.

As shown by the measures of long-range volatility dependence in Table 4.3, and in line with the graphical inspection and semiparametric estimations before, the memory parameters – see d_1 and d_2 in each column – do not seem to significantly depart much from each other.

To assess this conjecture, we now formally test whether any two fractional differencing parameters are statistically similar. The bivariate FIGARCH(1,d,1) specifications are constrained by imposing $d_1 = d_2$. The penultimate row of panel (a) in Table 4.5 shows the optimized mean log-likelihood of the constrained models. Except for the cases of Brazil–Venezuela and Mexico–Venezuela, a likelihood ratio cannot reject the hypothesis of common orders of fractional integration – see p-values in brackets.

In other words, despite the fact that each individual bond spread presumably follows its own individual volatility process, they both seem to be driven by a common information arrival process. This is consistent with the claim of Cunninham *et al.* (2001) who suggest that a single factor may drive all EBM spreads in the same direction. This finding also gives support to the view of Forbes and Rigobon (2000) for Latin American Brady markets in the sense that volatility is not driven by any individual country or subset of countries, but it is, instead, shared by all countries in the region. And finally, these conclusions add to the propositions of Kaminsky and Reinhart (2002) indicating that developed markets act as conduits between regions of developing countries.

4.4.2 Default risk contagion

The long-term time invariant comovement assumption may seem far too restrictive given the number of distress episodes observed in Latin America during the nineties. In fact, time varying cross correlations have already been found in stock and sovereign bond markets (see Hausler, 2003; Cunninham *et al.*, 2001).

Thus, to take this feature into account, in Table 4.4 we relax the constancy assumption and present the estimation results of the

Table 4.4 EMBI, unrestricted FIGARCH(1,*d*,1) QMLE estimations[a]

	(s_{art}, s_{brt})	(s_{art}, s_{mxt})	(s_{art}, s_{vet})	(s_{brt}, s_{mxt})	(s_{brt}, s_{vet})	(s_{mxt}, s_{vet})
Conditional mean						
μ_1	−0.0475	−0.0552	−0.0348	−0.0223	−0.0183	−0.0415
	(0.0250)	(0.0250)	(0.0251)	(0.0134)	(0.0133)	(0.0176)
μ_2	−0.0572	−0.0481	−0.0569	−0.0309	−0.0316	−0.0372
	(0.0189)	(0.0250)	(0.0231)	(0.0170)	(0.0191)	(0.0202)
Conditional variances						
ω_1	0.1133	0.1769	0.1549	0.0228	0.0223	0.0404
	(0.0112)	(0.0272)	(0.0269)	(0.0134)	(0.0050)	(0.0068)
β_1	0.4784	0.3588	0.2684	0.5063	0.5204	0.5483
	(0.0138)	(0.0807)	(0.0894)	(0.0603)	(0.0189)	(0.0176)
φ_1	0.3230	0.1809	0.0928	0.2946	0.3071	0.3121
	(0.0122)	(0.0703)	(0.0835)	(0.0581)	(0.0125)	(0.0136)
d_1	0.3539	0.3900	0.3019	0.3788	0.3858	0.3759
	(0.0245)	(0.0310)	(0.0268)	(0.0262)	(0.0251)	(0.0272)
ω_2	0.0748	0.1947	0.0972	0.0431	0.1007	0.1234
	(0.0131)	(0.0286)	(0.0188)	(0.0073)	(0.0149)	(0.0182)
β_2	0.1886	0.3424	0.4818	0.5456	0.4624	0.4395
	(0.0539)	(0.0733)	(0.0253)	(0.0202)	(0.0215)	(0.0224)
φ_2	0.0011	0.1454	0.3483	0.3018	0.3635	0.3768
	(0.0446)	(0.0601)	(0.0169)	(0.0152)	(0.0129)	(0.0123)
d_2	0.3441	0.4020	0.3034	0.3965	0.2729	0.2463
	(0.0232)	(0.0330)	(0.0338)	(0.0304)	(0.0258)	(0.0245)
Conditional covariance						
ω_{12}	0.0573	0.1282	0.0837	0.0149	0.0201	0.0369
	(0.0093)	(0.0181)	(0.0191)	(0.0052)	(0.0061)	(0.0096)
β_{12}	0.3599	0.3842	0.4348	0.2976	0.5134	0.5215
	(0.0299)	(0.0677)	(0.0650)	(0.0199)	(0.0168)	(0.0169)
φ_{12}	0.1971	0.2311	0.2819	0.3055	0.3576	0.3780
	(0.0310)	(0.0666)	(0.0626)	(0.0408)	(0.0110)	(0.0116)
d_{12}	0.3599	0.3391	0.2582	0.4989	0.2848	0.2439
	(0.0299)	(0.0260)	(0.0249)	(0.0448)	(0.0220)	(0.0233)

[a] See notes in Table 4.3.

unrestricted bivariate FIGARCH(1,*d*,1) model introduced in Equation 4.11 of Section 4. While the previous constant correlation model provided a good insight into the degree of association between any two bond spreads, the time variant specification will allow us to capture the extent of interdependence or fractional comovement in these markets.

The conditional covariance (h_{12}) is a measure of volatility in a given *portfolio*. It represents the risk perceived by the investor of holding two bonds. The joint long memory parameter, that is, d_{12}, indicates the extent of long-term default risk volatility contagion and, as shown, it is highly significant in all cases. We interpret *default risk contagion* as the situation in which the risk perception of default about one sovereign bond affects the risk perception of default of another bond in the same market.[19]

It is worth noticing in Table 4.4 that the orders of individual fractional integration, as well as their statistical significance, do not seem to be affected by the relaxation of the time invariant correlation assumption. What is more, the hypothesis of common long-range dependencies cannot be rejected. The optimized likelihood functions resulting from imposing the constraint $d_1 = d_2$ are presented in the fourth rows of panels (a) and (c) in Table 4.5 respectively and are labeled as $L(\theta)_{d_1=d_2}$. As indicated by the likelihood ratio (LR) tests – p-values in squared brackets – with the exception of the last two portfolios, sovereign bond spreads exhibit decay rates that are not statistically different from each other.

It was suggested in Section 4.2 that the decay rate of individual volatilities was different to that of the joint volatility measures. To test this conjecture we re-estimate the model in Equation 4.11 by imposing the restriction of common orders of fractional integration but now conditional covariances are included, that is, $d_1 = d_2 = d_{12}$. The row labeled $L(\theta)_{d_1=d_2=d_{12}}$ in panel (c) of Table 4.5 shows the optimized mean log-likelihood of these estimations. The results show a strong rejection of this hypothesis – see p-values of LR tests – indicating that even though countries may individually share the same degree of LM, interdependent shocks are propagated differently. That is, individual volatilities and volatility propagation in EBMs, that is, d_i and d_{ij}, may arise from different market sources.

4.4.3 The risk premium

Spreads in EBM are usually taken as measures of risk premium. However, spreads *per se* leave out the compensation required by investors for holding volatile sovereign instruments. Hence, to take this volatility component into account we now include the conditional

Table 4.5 EMBI, decision criteria FIGARCH(1,*d*,1) estimations

	(s_{art}, s_{brt})[a]	(s_{art}, s_{mxt})	(s_{art}, s_{vet})	(s_{brt}, s_{mxt})	(s_{brt}, s_{vet})	(s_{mxt}, s_{vet})
Panel (a): Brunetti CCC-FIGARCH (1,d,1)						
$L(\theta)$[b]	−4,911.3	−5,989.1	−5,361.4	−5,624.1	−5,391.9	−6,389.3
AIC[c]	9,844.6	12,000.3	10,744.7	11,270.3	10,805.9	12,800.7
SIC[d]	9,908.2	12,063.8	10,808.4	11,336.3	10,871.9	12,866.7
$L(\theta_{d_1=d_2})$[e]	−4,911.9	−5,991.3	−5,361.6	−5,624.3	−5,397.9	−6,393.9
LR[f]	(0.5488)[g]	(0.1108)	(0.8187)	(0.8190)	(0.0025)	(0.0101)
Panel (b): CCC-FIGARCH(1,d,1) variance in-mean						
$L(\theta)$	−4,906.0	−5,982.5	−5,654.7	−5,619.9	−5,386.4	−6,648.6
LR	(0.0314)[h]	(0.0103)	–	(0.0780)	(0.0266)	–
AIC	9,842.0	11,995.0	11,159.4	11,269.9	10,802.7	13,327.2
SIC	9,928.7	12,081.7	11,246.1	11,359.9	10,892.9	13,417.3
Panel (c): Unrestricted-FIGARCH(1,d,1)						
$L(\theta)$	−4,737.7	−5,794.5	−5,268.4	−5,524.4	−5,300.8	−6,342.7
AIC	9,503.5	11,617.0	10,564.8	11,076.8	10,629.6	12,713.4
SIC	9,584.4	11,697.9	10,645.8	11,160.9	10,713.7	12,797.5
$L(\theta_{d_1=d_2})$	−4,737.9	−5,794.5	−5,268.4	−5,524.5	−5,304.5	−6,347.8
LR	(0.4966)	(0.9999)	(0.9999)	(0.9048)	(0.0247)	(0.0074)
$L(\theta_{d_1=d_2=d_{12}})$	−4,810.3	−5,840.3	−5,275.3	−5,540.1	−5,309.4	−6,357.1
LR	–	(0.0001)	(0.0032)	(0.0000)	(0.0006)	(0.0001)
Panel (d): Unrestricted-FIGARCH(1,d,1) variance in-mean						
$L(\theta)$	−4,731.0	−5,786.4	−5,260.2	−5,519.1	−5,297.6	−6,339.5
LR	(0.0095)[i]	(0.0028)	(0.0025)	(0.0314)	(0.1712)	(0.1700)
AIC	9,498.1	11,608.8	10,556.5	11,074.2	10,631.2	12,715.0
SIC	9,602.1	11,712.9	10,660.5	11,182.4	10,739.4	12,823.2
Panel (e): Unrestricted-FIGARCH(1,d,1) covariance in-mean						
$L(\theta)$	−4,729.3	−5,787.4	−5,261.9	−5,522.4	−5,297.5	−6,339.9
LR	(0.0021)[i]	(0.0067)	(0.0113)	(0.4060)	(0.1586)	(0.2311)
AIC	9,495.2	11,610.8	10,559.9	11,080.9	10,630.5	12,715.7
SIC	9,598.7	11,714.9	10,663.9	11,188.9	10,739.2	12,823.9

[a] Subindex *i,j* indicate the bond components in a portfolio.
[b] Maximized Log-likelihood.
[c] Akaike information criteria.
[d] Schwartz information criterion.
[e] Maximized likelihood function with restriction in subindex.
[f] LR stands for likelihood ratio and is computed as $LR = -2\times[L(\theta_0) - L(\theta)]$ where $LR \sim \chi^2 m$ with m being to the number of linear restrictions.
[g] *p*-Values corresponding to the LR between the restricted model and the extended models respectively.
[h] *p*-Value of the LR between the in-mean version and the CCC-FIGARCH(1,*d*,1) model, panels (b) and (a) respectively.
[i] *p*-Value of the LR between the in-mean version and Teyssière FIGARCH(1,*d*,1) model, panels (d) and (e) against (c), respectively.

variances as regressors. The associated parameters can be interpreted as proxies for time varying risk premia.[20]

Tables 4.6 and 4.7 show mixed results with respect to the significance of individual risk premium estimates, see γ_{ij}. This seems consistent with Eichengreen and Moody (1998) who have suggested that individual risk premia often fail to reflect changing economic

Table 4.6 EMBI, CCC–FIGARCH(1,*d*,1) variance in-mean

	$(s_{art}, s_{brt})^a$	(s_{art}, s_{mxt})	(s_{art}, s_{vet})	(s_{brt}, s_{mxt})	(s_{brt}, s_{vet})	(s_{mxt}, s_{vet})
Conditional mean						
μ_1	−0.0963	−0.1320	−0.1336	−0.0429	−0.0849	−0.0655
	(0.0277)	(0.0305)	(0.0283)	(0.0173)	(0.0179)	(0.0211)
μ_2	−0.1057	−0.0917	−0.1162	−0.0473	−0.1131	−0.0698
	(0.0184)	(0.0299)	(0.0273)	(0.0233)	(0.0328)	(0.0252)
γ_{11}	0.0283	0.0289	0.0294	−0.0234	−0.0137	0.0082
	(0.0143)	(0.0165)	(0.0139)	(0.0288)	(0.0252)	(0.00147)
γ_{12}	0.0176	0.0205	0.0321	0.0293	0.0547	0.0139
	(0.0115)	(0.0127)	(0.0071)	(0.0142)	(0.0140)	(0.0071)
γ_{21}	0.0010	0.0025	−0.0004	0.0349	0.0009	0.0037
	(0.0049)	(0.0068)	(0.0051)	(0.0278)	(0.0258)	(0.0097)
γ_{22}	0.0519	0.0203	0.0487	−0.0106	0.0644	0.0289
	(0.0189)	(0.0164)	(0.0167)	(0.0227)	(0.0315)	(0.0186)
Conditional variances						
ω_1	0.1426	−0.0917	0.1236	0.0327	0.0363	0.0591
	(0.0134)	(0.0299)	(0.0124)	(0.0058)	(0.0058)	(0.0081)
β_1	0.4420	0.4741	0.4415	0.5002	0.4972	0.5041
	(0.0233)	(0.0755)	(0.0245)	(0.0220)	(0.0213)	(0.0528)
φ_1	0.3183	0.2586	0.3132	0.2858	0.2981	0.2749
	(0.0183)	(0.0589)	(0.0187)	(0.0147)	(0.0143)	(0.0464)
d_1	0.3634	0.4599	0.3736	0.4284	0.4037	0.4429
	(0.0366)	(0.0458)	(0.0373)	(0.0294)	(0.0286)	(0.0346)
ω_2	0.0929	0.1379	0.1653	0.0513	0.1567	0.1813
	(0.0179)	(0.0177)	(0.0218)	(0.0076)	(0.0207)	(0.0177)
β_2	0.2093	0.6167	0.3278	0.5442	0.3976	0.2958
	(0.1279)	(0.0597)	(0.0287)	(0.0229)	(0.0239)	(0.0242)
φ_2	0.0593	0.1399	0.3338	0.2968	0.3854	0.3561
	(0.1115)	(0.0377)	(0.0168)	(0.0176)	(0.0125)	(0.0131)
d_2	0.4169	0.6631	0.3324	0.4064	0.2293	0.2879
	(0.0349)	(0.0715)	(0.0337)	(0.0351)	(0.0249)	(0.0262)
ρ_{12}	0.7154	0.6088	0.5943	0.5198	0.5627	0.4982
	(0.0053)	(0.0080)	(0.0089)	(0.0099)	(0.0108)	(0.0101)

[a] See notes in Table 4.3.

Table 4.7 EMBI, unrestricted FIGARCH(1,*d*,1) variance-in-mean

	(s_{art}, s_{brt})[a]	(s_{art}, s_{mxt})	(s_{art}, s_{vet})	(s_{brt}, s_{mxt})	(s_{brt}, s_{vet})	(s_{mxt}, s_{vet})
Conditional mean						
μ_1	−0.1063	−0.1556	−0.1712	−0.0598	−0.0652	−0.0759
	(0.0307)	(0.0317)	(0.0400)	(0.0213)	(0.0196)	(0.0267)
μ_2	−0.1169	−0.1115	−0.1832	−0.0605	−0.0920	−0.1165
	(0.0234)	(0.0329)	(0.0387)	(0.0268)	(0.0303)	(0.0339)
γ_{11}	0.0249	0.0294	0.0479	−0.0139	−0.0084	0.0163
	(0.0153)	(0.0154)	(0.0218)	(0.0298)	(0.0254)	(0.0211)
γ_{12}	0.0262	0.0273	0.0472	0.0338	0.0429	0.0136
	(0.0197)	(0.0121)	(0.0286)	(0.0149)	(0.0170)	(0.0231)
γ_{21}	0.0013	−0.0001	0.0149	0.0439	0.0102	0.0139
	(0.0062)	(0.0083)	(0.0127)	(0.0308)	(0.0274)	(0.0168)
γ_{22}	0.0656	0.0479	0.0779	−0.0087	0.0405	0.0502
	(0.0184)	(0.0366)	(0.0271)	(0.0230)	(0.0304)	(0.0292)
Conditional variances						
ω_1	0.1116	0.1709	0.1490	0.0243	0.0227	0.0408
	(0.0111)	(0.0262)	(0.0269)	(0.0089)	(0.0050)	(0.0068)
β_1	0.4788	0.3639	0.2550	0.4872	0.5186	0.5479
	(0.0140)	(0.0839)	(0.0947)	(0.0809)	(0.0189)	(0.0178)
φ_1	0.3237	0.1883	0.0847	0.2812	0.3114	0.3127
	(0.0125)	(0.0728)	(0.0878)	(0.0740)	(0.0125)	(0.0140)
d_1	0.3526	0.3884	0.2939	0.3685	0.3772	0.3746
	(0.0250)	(0.0323)	(0.0269)	(0.0354)	(0.0249)	(0.0281)
ω_2	0.0703	0.1832	0.0908	0.0436	0.0991	0.1191
	(0.0127)	(0.0276)	(0.0192)	(0.0114)	(0.0150)	(0.0183)
β_2	0.1984	0.3638	0.4811	0.5433	0.4632	0.4436
	(0.0538)	(0.0693)	(0.0243)	(0.0242)	(0.0211)	(0.0222)
φ_2	0.0146	0.1649	0.3535	0.3016	0.3644	0.3774
	(0.0453)	(0.0571)	(0.0163)	(0.0173)	(0.0128)	(0.0122)
d_2	0.3393	0.3992	0.2930	0.3965	0.2713	0.2451
	(0.0237)	(0.0339)	(0.0326)	(0.0346)	(0.0256)	(0.0244)
Conditional covariance						
ω_{12}	0.0555	0.1152	0.0785	0.0162	0.0205	0.0370
	(0.0086)	(0.0165)	(0.0191)	(0.0081)	(0.0061)	(0.0096)
β_{12}	0.3618	0.4258	0.4308	0.4850	0.5123	0.5215
	(0.0301)	(0.0614)	(0.0692)	(0.0596)	(0.0168)	(0.0168)
φ_{12}	0.1998	0.2687	0.2855	0.2921	0.3597	0.3789
	(0.0319)	(0.0628)	(0.0668)	(0.0536)	(0.0110)	(0.0117)
d_{12}	0.3072	0.3419	0.2502	0.2952	0.2807	0.2422
	(0.0194)	(0.0268)	(0.0245)	(0.0260)	(0.0219)	(0.0234)

[a] See notes in Table 4.3.

conditions and to respond to changes in the spreads of other countries. Nonetheless, LR tests against the no in-mean specifications – see panels (a) to (d) in Table 4.5 – and SIC strongly confirm that time varying risk premia do *jointly* drive the behaviour of excess returns in EBMs.

Overall, and as it would be expected, during the period under analysis a greater volatility has been reflected in higher risk premia. The extent of individual risk premium in one market differs greatly from portfolio to portfolio. For instance, if we consider the portfolio Argentina–Brazil in the first column of Table 4.6,[21] we observe that the magnitude of the risk premium required to hold Argentinean bonds (γ_{11}) is equivalent to the size of the mean return standard deviation. Similarly, the risk premium for holding Brazilian bonds (γ_{22}) in this portfolio is equivalent to more than two standard deviations of its mean return. These magnitudes are quite substantial and indicate a stronger risk aversion by investors during the sample period.

Hence, holders of Argentinean bonds claimed a considerable premium for investing in its own instrument. However they might also have adjusted for the effect of holding Brazilian bonds in their portfolio. The cross effects (γ_{12}) measure the extra premium arising from holding the second bond in the portfolio.[22] The magnitude of (γ_{12}) in the first column of Table 4.6 indicates that the additional compensation required by Argentinean investors for holding Brazilian bonds is not only large – two-thirds of standard deviation of mean return – but also statistically significant. In contrast, Brazilian investors however do not significantly adjust their premiums to account for their Argentinean holdings, suggesting that cross premia are not necessarily symmetric.

Additionally, the risk premia here obtained could be interpreted as a broad estimate of the probability of default attached to EBMs. The substantial levels of compensation for investing in EBMs reflect the investors' perception of increased credit risk and could also show the high probability of default expected by the market during the sample period.[23]

4.4.4 In-mean shared default risk perceptions

The high frequency nature of our model has prevented us from including consumption, prices or other critical fundamentals as regressors in the mean equation. An alternative method of taking fundamentals into account has been proposed by Baillie and Bollerslev (1990) who have suggested the inclusion of the asset return covariances as proxies of the comovement between bond returns and consumption. In this section we follow this approach by including the conditional covariances as regressors.

The estimations of Equation 4.13 using covariances as well as the variance in-mean terms as regressors are shown in Table 4.8 where γ_{12} and γ_{21} now measure the impact of the covariances on excess returns. The results using these cross-premia proxies are at best weakly significant. In fact, from the information in panels (d) and (e) of Table 4.5, we observe that the only case in which there is a clear preference for covariance in-mean terms – as indicated by the optimized Likelihood value and Schwartz information criteria (SIC) – is in the portfolio Argentina–Brazil.[24]

The results seem to go in line with Eichengreen and Mody (1998) who have observed that changes in fundamentals, here proxied by conditional covariances, may only explain a fraction of spread compression in periods of crisis.

4.4.5 Econometric performance

Teyssière (1997, 1998) has shown that the optimized log-likelihood value of unrestricted bivariate FIGARCH(1,d,1) models is in general greater than the CCC-FIGARCH(1,d,1) of Brunetti and Christopher (2000). Selection criteria (AIC and SIC) overwhelmingly favour the unrestricted bivariate FIGARCH(1,d,1) model lending support for time varying correlation models. As can be observed in Table 4.5 this finding is verified for Latin American EBMs (compare panels (a) and (c)).

Interestingly, by comparing Teyssière (1998) and Brunetti and Christopher (2000) models against our in-mean versions we observe in general that the inclusion of in-mean terms improves the optimized likelihood value. Also, Schwartz information criterion (that penalizes the inclusion of additional parameters) strongly prefers our new in-mean models. We test the restriction H_0: $\gamma_{11} = \gamma_{12} = \gamma_{21} = \gamma_{22} = 0$ using standard LR tests and as it can be observed, there is a clear rejection of the null in favour of in-mean parameters, see p-values in brackets in panels (b) and (d), respectively.[25]

Table 4.8 EMBI, unrestricted FIGARCH(1,d,1) covariance-in-mean

	(s_{art}, s_{brt})[a]	(s_{art}, s_{mxt})	(s_{art}, s_{vet})	(s_{brt}, s_{mxt})	(s_{brt}, s_{vet})	(s_{mxt}, s_{vet})
Conditional mean						
μ_1	−0.1188	−0.1424	−0.1381	−0.0390	−0.0368	−0.0638
	(0.0306)	(0.0312)	(0.0378)	(0.0197)	(0.0173)	(0.0244)
μ_2	−0.1222	−0.0939	−0.1549	−0.0382	−0.0863	−0.1095
	(0.0231)	(0.0322)	(0.0368)	(0.0253)	(0.0305)	(0.0329)
γ_{11}	0.0450	0.0457	0.0409	−0.0303	−0.0777	0.0010
	(0.0219)	(0.0187)	(0.0255)	(0.0398)	(0.0429)	(0.0288)
γ_{12}	0.0080	0.0137	0.0543	0.0775	0.1499	0.0425
	(0.0355)	(0.0258)	(0.0501)	(0.0512)	(0.0592)	(0.0611)
γ_{21}	0.0700	0.0517	0.0396	0.0663	−0.0038	−0.0046
	(0.0317)	(0.0344)	(0.0485)	(0.0566)	(0.0556)	(0.0546)
γ_{22}	0.0031	−0.0058	0.0544	−0.0210	0.0508	0.0662
	(0.0346)	(0.0261)	(0.0395)	(0.0280)	(0.0382)	(0.0374)
Conditional variances						
ω_1	0.1127	0.1716	0.1553	0.0243	0.0242	0.0407
	(0.0112)	(0.0260)	(0.0275)	(0.0089)	(0.0057)	(0.0068)
β_1	0.4765	0.3657	0.2538	0.4904	0.5044	0.5482
	(0.0143)	(0.0821)	(0.0948)	(0.2812)	(0.0474)	(0.0178)
φ_1	0.3236	0.1899	0.0841	0.2812	0.2969	0.3121
	(0.0127)	(0.0715)	(0.0880)	(0.0739)	(0.0431)	(0.0139)
d_1	0.3528	0.3858	0.2946	0.3734	0.3776	0.3758
	(0.0253)	(0.0319)	(0.0271)	(0.0359)	(0.0266)	(0.0278)
ω_2	0.0712	0.1830	0.0947	0.0436	0.1004	0.1213
	(0.0128)	(0.0276)	(0.0193)	(0.0113)	(0.0150)	(0.0185)
β_2	0.1928	0.3727	0.4790	0.5451	0.4627	0.4414
	(0.0538)	(0.0697)	(0.0247)	(0.0243)	(0.0211)	(0.0222)
φ_2	0.0074	0.1731	0.3529	0.3011	0.3648	0.3784
	(0.0449)	(0.0580)	(0.0164)	(0.0174)	(0.0127)	(0.0122)
d_2	0.3412	0.4036	0.2942	0.3987	0.2704	0.2431
	(0.0237)	(0.0343)	(0.0329)	(0.0348)	(0.0254)	(0.0243)
Conditional covariance						
ω_{12}	0.0562	0.1168	0.0825	0.0162	0.0213	0.0372
	(0.0087)	(0.0165)	(0.0194)	(0.0082)	(0.0062)	(0.0096)
β_{12}	0.3581	0.4276	0.4312	0.4867	0.5121	0.5219
	(0.0302)	(0.0609)	(0.0692)	(0.0599)	(0.0166)	(0.0168)
φ_{12}	0.1974	0.2703	0.2867	0.2928	0.3587	0.3789
	(0.0319)	(0.0625)	(0.0668)	(0.0536)	(0.0110)	(0.0116)
d_{12}	0.3082	0.3428	0.2508	0.2971	0.2825	0.2420
	(0.0195)	(0.0269)	(0.0246)	(0.0263)	(0.0219)	(0.0233)

[a] See notes in Table 4.3.

Among the different proxies of risk premia AIC and SIC seem to prefer the variance-in-mean terms. The optimized Likelihood function however is greater for the unrestricted specifications.

In terms of stability, apart from risk premia, parameter estimates remain highly significant and the magnitudes and precision do not seem to be affected after the inclusion of in-mean terms. A simulation study is being undertaken in continuing work to assess the relative improvement/performance of the QMLE estimation of the fractional differencing parameters in small samples. The models are also extended to consider the effect of asymmetries in a bivariate FIEGARCH context.

4.5 Conclusions and discussion

The contribution of this chapter has been twofold: first we have uncovered the high degree of volatility persistency, strong fractional comovement and risk premia of Latin American EBMs and, second, we have proposed a new family of bivariate long memory models to capture these salient features. These new models not only allow to derive time varying estimates of volatilities, correlations and investors' risk aversion series, but also account for the high predictability observed in these markets.

Long memory in EBMs is explained as the result of financial market rigidities and informational deficiencies. A potential implication of this finding is that domestic policies, for example, capital controls, oriented at constraining the effect of sudden destabilization shocks may only be of temporary use. In line with the arguments of Forbes and Rigobon (2000) short-run isolation strategies may be costly and only delay a country's adjustment to equilibrium.

The results also suggest a high degree of *fractional comovement* in these markets. Default risk contagion parameters are in all cases highly significant. This outcome is consistent with the claims of Mauro *et al.* (2000), Fiess (2003) and Cunninham *et al.* (2001) who report strong comovement of spreads in EBMs.

We find that the individual degrees of LM are not statistically different from each other. This lends support to the conjecture that a common market factor drives EBM spreads. Episodes of contagion for instance may have a common base being either Brady markets (Baig and Goldfajn, 2000) or any other developed financial market acting as the conduit between regions of developing markets (Kaminsky and Reinhart, 2002). In order to deal with pervasive shocks, Latin American countries should then *coordinate* their efforts rather than cope with turmoils on an individual basis.

Derivative markets on these instruments are not still fully developed. For this reason, focusing on volatilities implicit in market prices of option-like credit derivatives would not be feasible. Bielcki and Rutowski (2003) have already observed that the valuation of credit derivatives requires to take into account credit spread volatilities and, if several distinct assets are modelled simultaneously, credit spread correlations. The models proposed here provide solid proxies for these variables.

In addition, policy makers and investors in Latin American sovereign bond markets might be interested in assessing the effect of contagious shocks on the volatility of its own market and on the market perception of default risk. The models presented here are capable of capturing such phenomena.

Another potential implication of the LM finding relates to the pricing of derivatives. Baillie *et al.* (1996) have already showed that valuation of derivatives under the presence of LM may be highly unreliable and heavy loses are possible. A future line of research should investigate the effect of LM in the valuation of sovereign basket derivatives.

Notes

The author would like to acknowledge the sharp comments and suggestions made by Prof. Peter N. Smith and Dr. Liudas Giraitis.

1. See Min (1998), Ferrucci (2003), Eichengreen and Moody (1998) and Fiess (2003).
2. A notable exception is Jostova (2002) who finds that credit spreads are non-stationary variables and from this carries out a cointegration analysis with fundamentals. Deviations from long-run equilibrium are then used to predict excess returns over US treasuries.
3. The data has been kindly provided by EcoWin.
4. The EMBI for each country is calculated as the weighted average spread of all Brady bonds with similar properties. For further discussion on the actual calculation of credit spreads see Jostova (2002).
5. Spreads also reflect various other risks: exchange rate risk, interest rate risk, liquidity risk and default risk. Benczur (2001) notices that the first of these should be almost nil, while liquidity risk is usually the result of market conditions, volatility components or asymmetries.
6. This conjecture is in direct contrast with the analysis of Forbes and Rigobon (2000) who by analyzing a shorter sample and the difference between any two given spreads suggested a relatively constant risk premium.

7. Credit risk in this context may be interpreted as a measure of a sovereign government's ability to meet its principal and/or interests.
8. Cunninham *et al.* (2001) have also noted this in their study.
9. Confidence intervals are depicted by the dotted lines and are calculated as $2/\sqrt{n}$ where n is the sample size.
10. The minimun transaction size in Brady markets is of US$2 million leaving room only to large investors such as mutual, endowment and pension funds (Jostova, 2002).
11. The tests include Lobato and Robinson (1998) *t*-test, the Modified Rescaled test of Lo (1991) and the rescaled variance V/S test of Giraitis *et al.* (2002). Estimation results and calculation details are available upon request.
12. Among other alternatives that generate slow decay of the ACF of returns are the two-component model of Ding and Granger (1993, 1996).
13. See Cunninham *et al.* (2001) and the Quarterly Global Financial Stability Report of the IMF for more on this. Previous litterature using correlation coefficients as measures of contagion include Forbes and Rigobon (1999, 2000).
14. Baig and Goldfajn (2000) suggest indeed that excluding volatilities from the analysis may be misleading. Contagion for instance is the result of panic, margin calls, thin markets, and such like factors which are at the same time responsible for changes in volatility.
15. Brunetti and Christopher (2000) used a bivariate CCC–FIGARCH framework to model fractional cointegration in oil markets.
16. For further discussion about robustness, consistency, ergodicity and asymptotic normality properties under this estimation method see Baillie *et al.* (1996).
17. We tried different FARIMA(p,d,q)–FIGARCH($1,d,1$) specifications and used the Log-likelihood value, Schwartz Information Criterion (SIC) and Akaike Information Criterion (AIC) to discriminate between models. As Teyssière (1997) points out, the statistical properties of the AIC and SIC have not been established for the class of LM ARCH process; however it is considered here that these statistics provide good reasonable guidance. They are calculated herein as:

$$\text{AIC} = -2\ln(L(\hat{\theta})) + 2^{*}n_{\theta}$$
$$\text{SIC} = -2\ln(L(\hat{\theta})) + n_{\theta}{}^{*}\ln(n)$$

    where $L(\hat{\theta})$ is the optimized likelihood value, n_{θ} is the number of estimated parameters and n is the sample size.
18. The initial estimation procedure was kindly provided by Celso Brunetti, University of Pennsylvania. The estimation strategy consisted in using starting values from univariate FIGARCH($1,d,1$) estimations. Convergence was achieved by reducing the effect of outliers to no more than three standard deviations. The original samples of Argentina–Brazil and Argentina–Mexico converged satisfactorily without adjusting outliers. In all the estimations we used BFGS optimization algorithm although estimations via BHHH were quite similar and usually less computing intensive.

19. Definitions for credit contagion can be found in Avellaneda and Wu (2001) or Giesecke and Weber (2003).
20. In addition to these specifications, we also considered the inclusion of two additional in-mean functions: $g = \sqrt{h_{it}}$ and $g = log(h_{it})$. Preliminary results suggest that the qualitative conclusions remain unchanged. Also, the squared root transformations seem to perform better than simple in-mean effects.
21. Similar conclusions may be drawn for the analysis of all the portfolios in Tables 4.6–4.8. We consider only one case to save space.
22. These could also be interpreted as short-term contagion measures.
23. This is a natural interpretation given the many events of financial distress, devaluations, defaults and crisis in Latin American markets during the end of the nineties.
24. The weak significance of these parameters is also in agreement with the results of Baillie and Bollerslev (1990).
25. Such testing framework however renders mixed results for the case of covariance in mean parameters. See panel (e).

References

Avellaneda, M. and L. Wu (2001), Credit contagion: pricing cross-country risk in Brady debt markets, *International Journal of Theoretical and Applied Finance* 4(6), 921–38.

Baig, T. and I. Goldfajn (2000), The Russian default and the contagion to Brazil, *IMF Working Papers* 160.

Baillie, R. and T. Bollerslev (1990), A multivariate generalized ARCH approach to modelling risk premia in forward foreign exchange markets, *Journal of International Money and Finance* 9, 309–24.

Baillie, R., T. Bollerslev and H. Mikkelsen (1996), Fractionally integrated generalized autoregressive conditional heteroskedasticity, *Journal of Econometrics* 74, 3–30.

Benczur, P. (2001), Learning, noise traders, the volatility and the level of Bond Spreads, in *Proceedings Summer Workshop*, Institute of Economics, Hungarian Academy of Sciences.

Bielecki, T. and M. Rutkowski (2003), Dependent defaults and credit migrations, *Applicationes Mathematicae* 30, 121–45.

Bollerslev, T. (1986), A generalized autoregressive conditional heteroskedasticity, *Journal of Econometrics* 31, 307–27.

Bollerslev, T. (1990), Modeling the coherence in the short-run nominal exchange rates: a multivariate generalized ARCH model, *Review of Economics and Statistics* 72, 498–505.

Bollerslev, T. and H. Mikkelsen (1996), Modeling and pricing long memory in stock market volatility, *Journal of Econometrics* 73, 151–84.

Bollerslev, T. and J. M. Wooldridge (1992), Quasi maximum likelihood estimation and inference in a dynamic model with time varying covariances, *Econometric Review* 11, 143–72.

Bougerol, P. and N. Picard (1992), Stationarity of GARCH processes and some nonnegative time series, *Journal of Econometrics* 52, 115–28.
Brunetti, C. and L. Christopher (2000), Bivariate FIGARCH and fractional cointegration, *Journal of Empirical Finance* 7, 509–30.
Cunninham, A., L. Dixon and S. Hayes (2001), Analysing yield spreads on emerging market sovereign bonds, *Financial Stability Review*, Bank of England December.
Ding, Z. and C. Granger (1996), Modeling volatility persistence of speculative returns: A new approach, *Journal of Econometrics* 73, 185–215.
Eichengreen, B. and A. Mody (1998), What explains changing srpeads on emerging market debt: fundamentals or market sentiment, *NBER Working Papers* 6408.
Engle, R. and T. Bollerslev (1986), Modeling the persistence of conditional variances, *Econometric Review* 5, 81–7.
Ferrucci, G. (2003), Empirical determinants of sovereign EMEs bond spreads, Bank of England *Mimeo*.
Fiess, N. (2003), Capital flows, country risk and contagion, *World Bank Working Papers* 2943.
Forbes, K. and R. Rigobon (1999), No contagion, only Interdependence: Measuring stock market comovements, *NBER Working Papers* 7267.
Forbes, K. and R. Rigobon (2000), Contagion in Latin America: definitions, measurement and policy implications, *NBER Working Papers* 7885.
Giesecke, K. and S. Weber (2003), Credit contagion and aggregate losses, Cornell University and Stefan Weber of the Technische Universität Berlin. http://www.defaultrisk.com/pp_corr_33.htm.
Giraitis, L., R. Leipus and A. Philippe (2002), The test for stationary versus trends and unit roots for a wide class of dependent errors, *Laboratoire de Mathémathiques Appliquées*, CNRS FRE 222.
Hausler, G. (2003), Global financial stability report, market developments and issues, *World Economic and Financial Surveys*, IMF Several issues.
Jostova, G. (2002), Predictability in emerging sovereign debt markets, in Proceedings of the Midwestern Finance Association.
Kaminsky, G. and C. Reinhart (2002), The center and the periphery: the globalization of financial turmoil, Paper presented at the Third Joint Central Bank Research Conference on Risk Measurement and Systemic Risk, BIS, Basel, Switzerland, pp. 7–8.
Lobato, I. and P. Robinson (1998), A nonparametric test for I(0), *The Review of Economic Studies* 65(3), 475–95.
Mauro, P., N. Sussman and Y. Yafeh (2000), Emerging market spreads: then versus now, *IMF Working Papers* WP/00/190.
Min, H. (1998), Determinants of emerging market bond spread: do economic fundamentals matter? *World Bank Working Papers* 1899.
Nelson, D. (1991), Conditional heteroskedasticity in asset returns: a new approach, *Econometrica* 59, 347–70.
Teyssière, G. (1997), Modeling exchange rates volatility with multivariate long-memory ARCH processes, *GREQAM* 97B03.
Teyssière, G. (1998), Multivariate long-memory ARCH modeling for high frequency foreign exchange rates, *GREQAM* 98.

5
Econometric Modelling of the Euro Using Two-Factor Continuous Time Dynamic Interest Rate Models

Khalid B. Nowman and Harry Thapar

5.1 Introduction

The introduction of the Euro and the development of financial instruments based on Euro interest rates has become an important research area. There are now many bonds in the Eurozone area whose pricing depends on the specification of a model of interest rates. In this chapter we consider the modelling of Euro interest rates using well-known continuous time interest rate models. There exist many different models of the short-term interest rate, and the usual starting-point is the single-factor model of Chan, Karolyi, Longstaff and Sanders (1992, CKLS hereafter), which included many special cases. Two of these special cases are the models of Vasicek (1977) and Cox, Ingersoll and Ross (1985, CIR hereafter), which are used in this chapter. The application of Gaussian estimation econometric methods of Bergstrom (1983, 1990) with available discrete data was considered recently in Nowman (1997) to these single-factor models for the United States of America and the United Kingdom. It was shown for the United States of America that there was a strong relationship between the volatility of rates and the level of rates, as was originally found in CKLS. Nowman (1997) found the opposite for the United Kingdom. More recently Nowman (2001) extended the Gaussian estimation of single-factor models to estimate two-factor CKLS, Vasicek and CIR models and an application to Japan indicated that the Vasicek model performs the best and for the United Kingdom the CIR model. In this study we apply Nowman (2001) to weekly Euro interest rates. We find that there is a strong relationship between the volatility of rates and the level of rates for the 1-month rate compared to the 1-year rate and that the CIR model performs the best.

The chapter is organized as follows: Section 5.2 discusses the continuous time models and the two-factor Gaussian estimation method of Nowman (2001). Section 5.3 presents the data and Section 5.4 the empirical results. The final section concludes the chapter.

5.2 CKLS, Vasicek and CIR models and estimation

In this section we discuss the continuous time interest rate models starting with the CKLS and the special cases we consider. The CKLS model of the short-term interest rate is represented by Equation 5.1 below. The equation allows the conditional mean and variance to depend on the level r

$$dr(t) = \{\alpha + \beta r(t)\}dt + \sigma r^{\gamma}(t)d\zeta(t) \quad (t \geq 0) \tag{5.1}$$

where $\{r(t),\ t > 0\}$ is the short-term interest rate, α and β are the unknown drift and mean reversion structural parameters; σ is the volatility of the short-term rate and γ is the proportional volatility exponent. The error term is usually assumed to be a Wiener process. Nowman (2001) considered the following two-factor CKLS version with correlated factors given by Equations 5.2 and 5.3:

$$dr_1(t) = \{\alpha_1 + \beta_1 r_1(t)\}dt + \zeta_1(dt) \quad (t \geq 0) \tag{5.2}$$

$$dr_2(t) = \{\alpha_2 + \beta_2 r_2(t)\}dt + \zeta_2(dt) \quad (t \geq 0) \tag{5.3}$$

where $r_1(t)$ and $r_2(t)$ represented the short- and long-term interest rates and α_1, α_2, β_1 and β_2 are the drift and mean reversion parameters. Nowman (2001) assumed the error terms satisfied Assumption 1:

Assumption 1 (Nowman, 2001): ζ_1 and ζ_2 are random measures defined on all subsets of the half line $0 < t < \infty$ with finite Lebesgue measure, such that: $E[\zeta_1(dt)] = 0$, $E[\zeta_2(dt)] = 0$ and $E[\zeta_1(dt)\zeta_2(dt)] = (dt)\Sigma(r,t)$, where $\Sigma(r,t)$ was a positive definite matrix assumed in Nowman (2001, equation 4) to be:

$$\sum(r, t) = \begin{bmatrix} \sigma_1^2 r_1^{2\gamma_1}(t) & \rho_{12}\sigma_1\sigma_2 r_1^{\gamma_1}(t) r_2^{\gamma_2}(t) \\ \rho_{21}\sigma_2\sigma_1 r_2^{\gamma_2}(t) r_1^{\gamma_1}(t) & \sigma_2^2 r_2^{2\gamma_2}(t) \end{bmatrix} \tag{5.4}$$

The assumption used in CKLS for the single factor is represented by the first element. Nowman (2001) used the same assumption for the second factor but allowed them to be correlated. Nowman (2001) then used the assumption of constant volatility over the unit observation period applied to Equation 5.4 as used in the single factor model case in Nowman (1997) to estimate the two-factor versions of the CKLS, Vasicek ($\gamma_1 = 0$, $\gamma_2 = 0$) and CIR ($\gamma_1 = 0.5$, $\gamma_2 = 0.5$) models. The discrete model of Nowman (2001, equation 6) is given below.

$$r_t = e^{\beta} r_{t-1} + (e^{\beta} - I)\beta^{-1}\alpha + \varepsilon_t \quad (t = 1,2, \ldots ,T) \tag{5.5}$$

where

$$e^{\beta} = I + \sum_{i=1}^{\infty} \frac{1}{i!} \beta^i$$

$$E(\varepsilon_t \varepsilon_t') = \int_0^1 e^{r\beta} \sum{}^{*} (r, t) e^{r\beta'} \, dr = \Omega(r, t)$$

$$\alpha = \begin{bmatrix} \alpha_1 \\ \alpha_2 \end{bmatrix}, \quad \beta = \begin{bmatrix} \beta_1 & 0 \\ 0 & \beta_2 \end{bmatrix}$$

and Σ^* has the same general form as Equation 5.4 (see Nowman, 2001). Nowman (2001, equation 7) then obtained the Gaussian estimates from the Gaussian likelihood function below:

$$L(\theta) = \sum_{t=1}^{T} \log(|\Omega(r, t)|) + \sum_{t=1}^{T} \varepsilon_t' \Omega^{-1}(r, t) \varepsilon_t \tag{5.6}$$

5.3 The data

The interest rate used in this study is the weekly one and 12-month Euro interbank rates extracted from the Datastream database over the period January 1999 to June 2004 giving a total of 283 observations. Table 5.1 shows the basic summary statistics. The average level of the 1- and 12-month rates are 3.49 and 3.65 per cent respectively, with standard deviations of 0.837 and 0.893 per cent. The first six autocorrelations of the levels decay slowly and the first differences are

Table 5.1 Summary data statistics: January 1999–June 2004

Variable	Mean	SD	ρ_1	ρ_2	ρ_3	ρ_4	ρ_5	ρ_6	ADF
1M									
$r(t)$	3.4948	0.8372	0.99	0.97	0.96	0.95	0.93	0.92	−0.3445
$\Delta r(t)$	−0.0044	0.0779	0.14	0.15	0.02	0.02	0.05	0.05	−13.763
12M									
$r(t)$	3.6488	0.8936	0.99	0.98	0.97	0.95	0.93	0.92	−1.0191
$\Delta r(t)$	−0.0037	0.0841	0.14	0.13	0.13	0.02	0.08	0.08	−13.785

Mean, standard deviations and autocorrelations of weekly interest rate. The variable $r(t)$ is the level and $\Delta r(t)$ is the daily change, ρ_j is the autocorrelation coefficient of order j. ADF denotes the augmented Dickey–Fuller unit root statistic.

small. The (ADF) statistics do not reject the null hypothesis of a unit root in the level series.

Figures 5.1 and 5.2 show the historic Euro interbank rates. Broadly the pattern could be delineated into two; in the first phase the European Central Bank (ECB) was pursuing a tighter monetary policy stance and, during the second phase, to date, when monetary policy is relaxed has remained more accommodative. In the first phase, the Euro came under selling pressure as a result of the market's lack of confidence in the newly introduced currency. The ECB was under test and resisted the temptation to raise interest rates initially just to support the ailing currency and to bolster its credibility with the markets. ECB made it clear that it targeted inflation, not exchange rates. It was however justified in tightening monetary policy in 2000. Germany, the Eurozone's biggest economy was expected to grow by 3 per cent in 2000 (compared to 1.5 per cent in the previous year). The growth had been boosted by a weak Euro and a recovering global economy. Both the United States of America and the United Kingdom were already tightening monetary policy. ECB started to raise interest rates in early 2000, on clear signs that Europe had come out of an economic slowdown, with oil prices surging above the US$30 a barrel and inflation in the 11-nation Eurozone was reaching 2 per cent (top of the ECB target zone of 0–2 per cent). In the second phase, the Euro had recovered against the dollar and there were tentative signs that the ECB would have to lower rates. By 2001, there were clear signs that the Eurozone's economy had slowed. Basically, this was due to a slowdown in the USA and a series of mostly global, common shocks that have spread throughout the world economy with surprising

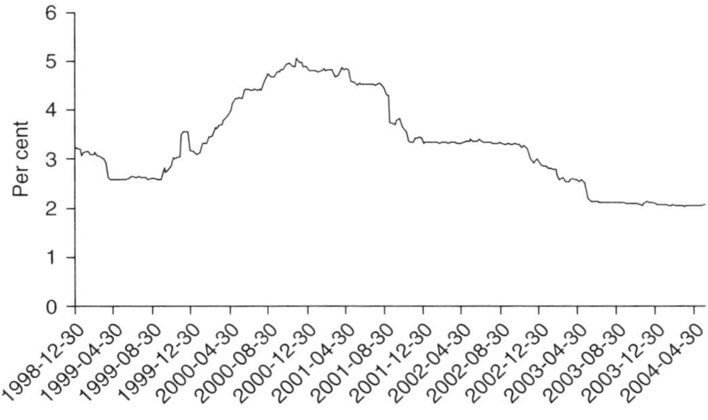

Figure 5.1 Euro 1-month interbank rate

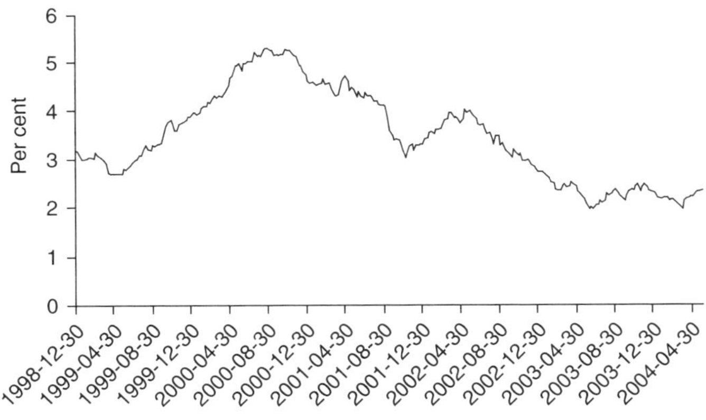

Figure 5.2 Euro 12-month interbank rate

speed, including the euro area. At this point, risks of a more severe downturn and a sharper increase in unemployment were significant. Domestic demand in the area's largest economy seemed to be particularly hard hit and there was a danger that the Eurozone economy was vulnerable to external shocks. In this evolving and difficult environment, inflation pressures moderated and the downward momentum of the cyclical economic slowdown was apparent. ECB loosened monetary policy decisively following the events of September 11. In the following months rates were lowered gradually and monetary policy remained accommodative. After cutting interest rates the ECB held its interest rate on hold at 2 per cent since June 2003. ECB was however prepared to ease if the projected recovery of domestic demand did not materialize and, so long as the outlook for price stability remained benign.

5.4 Empirical results

We now discuss the Gaussian estimates (standard errors in brackets) of the two-factor term structure models presented in Table 5.2. Following Nowman (1997, 2001) the explanatory power of each model is compared to the unrestricted model using the maximized Gaussian log-likelihood function value. Based on the maximized

Table 5.2 Gaussian estimates of two-factor models

Parameters	CKLS	Vasicek	CIR
α_1	−0.0001	−0.0001	−0.0001
	(0.0001)	(0.0001)	(0.0001)
α_2	0.0002	0.0002	0.0002
	(0.0001)	(0.0002)	(0.0002)
β_1	0.0005	0.0013	0.0010
	(0.0048)	(0.0054)	(0.0046)
β_2	−0.0067	−0.0065	−0.0066
	(0.0050)	(0.0060)	(0.0051)
γ_1	1.1743	0.0	0.5
	(0.1906)		
γ_2	0.3532	0.0	0.5
	(0.1424)		
σ_2^1	0.0015	0.0000*	0.0001
	(0.0020)	(0.0000*)	(0.0000*)
σ_2^2	0.0000*	0.0000*	0.0002
	(0.0000*)	(0.0000*)	(0.0000*)
ρ_{12}	0.4746	0.5017	0.4782
	(0.0465)	(0.0469)	(0.0460)
Log LF	**1913.5186**	**1904.2645**	**1910.1085**
χ^2 ***test***		**18.5082**	**6.8202**

* Less than 0.0000.

Gaussian log-likelihood values compared to the unrestricted two-factor CKLS model the two-factor CIR model performs the best followed by the two-factor Vasicek model. Regarding the unrestricted model, the Gaussian estimates of γ_1 and γ_2 are 1.1743 and 0.3532 for the 1-month and 1-year rates. In Nowman (2001) for Japan it was found that the Vasicek model performs the best followed by the CIR model and for the UK, the CIR model followed by the Vasicek model. There is no evidence of mean reversion in the interest rates. Given that the Euro is so new, we have not built up a long enough history about interest rates so that the lack of evidence of mean reversion is what is to be expected. In contrast, Nowman (2001) found that there was weak evidence of mean reversion in the 1-month rate compared to the 1-year rate. The correlation parameter indicates 47–50 per cent between the two factors in the models. Based on the χ^2 likelihood ratio test under the null hypothesis that the nested models' restrictions are valid the results imply that we can reject the two-factor Vasicek and CIR models.

5.5 Conclusions

In this chapter we have estimated two-factor CKLS, Vasicek and CIR continuous time models of interest rates using the Gaussian estimation methods of Nowman (1977, 2001). These models differ in their relationship between the level of interest rates and the volatility of rates. The correct specification for this is important for implied bond pricing. Our empirical results indicate that for the Euro there is a strong relationship between the volatility of rates and the level of rates for the 1-month rate compared to the 1-year rate. This will have implications for the choice of model in Euro denominated financial markets.

References

Bergstrom, A. R. (1983), Gaussian estimation of structural parameters in higher-order continuous time dynamic models, *Econometrica* 51, 117–52.

Bergstrom, A. R. (1990), *Continuous Time Econometric Modelling*, Oxford University Press, Oxford.

Chan, K. C., G. A. Karolyi, F. A. Longstaff and A. B. Sanders (1992), An empirical comparison of alternative models of the short-term interest rate, *Journal of Finance* 47, 1209–27.

Cox, J. C., J. E. Ingersoll and S. Ross (1985), A theory of the term structure of interest rates, *Econometrica* 53, 385–407.

Nowman, K. B. (1997), Gaussian estimation of single-factor continuous time models of the term structure of interest rates, *Journal of Finance* 52, 1695–706.

Nowman, K. B. (2001), Gaussian estimation and forecasting of multi-factor term structure models with an application to Japan and the United Kingdom, *Asia Pacific Financial Markets* 8, 23–34.

Vasicek, O. (1977), An equilibrium characterization of the term structure, *Journal of Financial Economics* 5, 177–88.

6

Inflation Targeting in Emerging Economies: A Comparative Sacrifice Ratio Analysis

Rebeca I. Muñoz Torres

6.1 Introduction

In recent years, inflation targeting (IT) has emerged as the leading framework for monetary policy around the world.[1] The aim of inflation targeting is to contain inflationary expectations and enhance accountability regarding monetary policy by making a numerical target a medium-term objective. A growing number of studies have evaluated the performance of IT for industrialized countries (see Laubach and Posen, 1997; Bernanke *et al.*, 1999; Honda, 2000), but little attention has been given to emerging economies (see Bogdanski *et al.*, 2000; Leiderman and Bufman, 2000; Fraga *et al.*, 2003). Countries such as Brazil, Chile, the Czech Republic, Israel, Mexico and South Africa implemented IT during the 1990s. Some of these emerging economies have been forced to implement most of the IT requirements as a consequence of serious financial crises (see Masson *et al.*, 1997; Agénor, 2000; Schaechter *et al.*, 2000).[2] However, they have followed successful strategies for disinflation during the transition towards a fully fledged IT regime.[3]

This chapter considers a sample of emerging economies with moderate and high levels of inflation that have followed different strategies for disinflation. These countries are divided into two categories according to the monetary policy regime under which they have attempted to reduce inflation: (1) countries that have adopted an IT regime and (2) countries with another monetary policy framework. The main objective is to assess the effectiveness of IT by estimating sacrifice ratios using three alternative approaches. First, actual changes in inflation are compared with changes in standard measures of output. Second, the sacrifice ratio is estimated using the Phillips curve approach to capture the output–inflation trade off for a given time period. Third, following Cecchetti and Rich (2001) estimates of the sacrifice ratio are derived using a structural vector autoregressive (VAR) model. A summary of the results shows that for countries where the process of disinflation has been accompanied by the adoption of IT, sacrifice ratios have either increased less or declined over time. Moreover, these countries seem to have lower and more stable levels of inflation.

The structure of this chapter is as follows: Section 2 presents a brief review of the literature on IT and its implications in terms of disinflation focusing on both industrialized and emerging economies. Section 3 describes the methodological approaches and data used in this chapter. Section 4 discusses the empirical results. General conclusions are given in the final section.

6.2 Background

A vast amount of research on IT has been carried out in recent years, mainly for industrialized countries. These studies have examined a range of aspects of IT, such as the rationale for IT (e.g. McCallum, 1996; Debelle, 1997; Kuttner and Posen, 1999; Mishkin and Schmidt-Hebbel, 2002), implementation issues (e.g. Haldane, 1995; Bernanke and Mishkin, 1997; Schaechter *et al.*, 2000) and IT as an alternative to the use of monetary targets (e.g. Mishkin, 1997; Groeneveld *et al.*, 1998). However, the empirical findings on the effectiveness of IT remain unclear. A recent study by Mishkin and Posen (1997) examined the experience of the first three industrialized countries to adopt IT, New Zealand, Canada and Sweden. They suggest that these countries have successfully maintained low inflation rates along with an improvement in the climate for economic growth. Similar conclusions arise from a study by McCallum (1996), who compared the inflation performance for New Zealand, Canada, Sweden and the United Kingdom, with an average of CPI inflation rates across 23 industrialized nations. In contrast, there are a number of studies arguing that the performance of IT has not been clearly successful which will be briefly discussed later.

Lee (1999) examined whether regime effects, such as inflation reductions, have been associated with a global disinflationary environment rather than the implementation of IT. He found that the sustained reduction of inflation rates in targeting countries could have been achieved in the absence of IT.[4] Another study by Groeneveld *et al.* (1998), which evaluated the success of IT in Canada, New Zealand and the United Kingdom found similar results of inflation and interest rate instability with a group of non-IT countries (the United States of America, Australia and Germany). In the same way, an earlier study by Laubach and Posen (1997) with a sample of eight industrialized countries threw doubt on the successfulness of IT. They evaluated whether IT achieves positive results with less cost in terms of output or in terms of maintainable expectations. Using sacrifice ratios and forecasts from Phillips curves, they suggest that disinflation under IT is not less costly than without it.

Turning to emerging economies, a few studies have been carried out which make drawing conclusions difficult. Studies including those by Leiderman and Bufman (2000), Schaechter *et al.* (2000), Bogdanski *et al.* (2000) and Masson *et al.* (1997) mainly summarize the institutional and operational practicalities of IT without considering econometric specifications. The lack of substantial empirical work may be explained due to the recent adoption of IT by emerging economies. Therefore, the debate mainly focuses on technical issues regarding how IT should be practised in emerging economies, and whether the existence of such a regime has been beneficial for these countries (see Fraga *et al.*, 2003; Reyes, 2003). Interestingly, Corbo *et al.* (2001, 2002) suggest that a large number of questions on the results of IT remain unanswered. Their investigation provides a wide empirical analysis on the rationale and consequences of adopting IT by comparing policies and outcomes in fully fledged IT countries with two control groups of potential targeters and non-targeters.[5] They reported that inflation persistence declined sharply among IT countries, suggesting that this regime played an important role in strengthening the effects of forward-looking expectations on inflation. Furthermore, they showed that output volatility had fallen in both emerging and industrialized economies after adopting IT.

One way to measure the effectiveness of IT is to compare sacrifice ratios among countries or/and among different sample periods. It is widely accepted by economists that lower inflation rates give rise to long-run benefits for society. However, there is also a strong belief that conducting monetary policy to slow down inflation involves some short-run cost in terms of loss in output, namely, the *sacrifice ratio* (see Mayes and Chapple, 1995). Although there are a number of studies analysing the cost of disinflation, the majority of them focus on industrialized countries (see Hutchinson and Walsh, 1998; Andersen and Wascher, 1999) and little information is known in the case of emerging economies. This chapter attempts to shed more light on the issue by estimating and comparing sacrifice ratios for 11 emerging economies with and without the adoption of IT during their process of achieving stable levels of inflation. Three alternative methods have been used to estimate sacrifice ratios in order to compensate the possible shortcomings of each of them.[6] First, disinflationary episodes for individual countries are identified and the sacrifice ratio for each period is calculated (see Andersen, 1992; Ball, 1994). Second, Phillips curves are estimated to derive the output–inflation trade off (see Blanchard, 1984; Hutchinson and Walsh, 1998). Finally, following Cecchetti and Rich (2001) a structural VAR is considered. The following section discusses each approach from a more analytical perspective and also the data used for this chapter.

6.3 Methods and data used

6.3.1 Methodology

6.3.1.1 Sacrifice ratios during episodes of disinflation

Ball (1994) identified disinflationary episodes for individual countries and calculated the sacrifice ratio for each period as the cumulative deviation of output from its equilibrium level divided by the permanent decline in inflation.[7] The sacrifice ratio is interpreted as the cost of reducing inflation one point through an aggregate demand contraction.[8] More specifically, he defines trend inflation as a centred nine-quarter moving average of actual inflation. Then he identifies peaks as quarters in which trend inflation is higher than in the previous and the following four quarters. A trough is defined by an analogous comparison. A disinflation episode is any period that starts at an inflation peak and ends at a trough with an annual inflation rate at least two points lower than the peak (see Ball, 1994). This method is relatively transparent, intuitive and one of the most frequently used. Cross-section studies, for example, using this technique commonly find that low inflation countries, or those with relatively independent central banks tend to have comparatively high sacrifice ratios (see Laubach and Posen, 1997; Andersen and Wascher, 1999; Bernanke *et al.*, 1999; Sanchez *et al.*, 1999).

One of the main issues involved in using this approach is the measurement of the potential output. To calculate the output losses associated with each disinflation episode the criteria used by Ball (1994) are adopted. Hence, the following three assumptions are considered:

1. The output is at its potential level at the inflation peak.
2. Output returns to its natural level one year after the end of the episode (i.e. four quarters after an inflation trough).
3. Trend output grows log-linearly between the two points where actual and trend output is the same. Geometrically, trend output is the straight line connecting these two points.

6.3.1.2 Sacrifice ratios estimated from the aggregate supply curve

The Phillips curve represents the relationship between the output or unemployment gap and inflation or wage inflation.[9] The key assumption behind the Phillips curve is that inflation depends on three key economic factors: (1) inflation expectations, (2) resource utilization pressures and (3) supply shocks (see Filardo, 1998). The latter overcomes one of the weaknesses of the previous method. The basic linear Phillips curve can be described algebraically as follows:

$$\pi_t = \pi_t^e + \lambda(y_t - y_t^*) + \varepsilon_t \tag{6.1}$$

or equivalently, as

$$y_t = y_t^* + \left(\frac{1}{\lambda}\right)\left[\pi_t - \pi_t^e - \varepsilon_t\right] \tag{6.2}$$

where inflation (π_t) is the percentage change in the aggregate price level, expected inflation (π_t^e) is a forecast at $t - 1$ of inflation at time t, the output gap ($y_t - y_t^*$) is a measure of the cyclical strength of the economy, and supply shocks (ε_t) are other factors that have temporary effects on inflation (e.g. through oil shocks and exchange rate changes). The coefficient λ, which is expected to have a positive value, measures the sensitivity of inflation to changes in the output gap.[10] In other words, λ is the trade off between output and inflation.

In this paper, however, the following specification of the Phillips curve is considered:

$$\pi_t = \alpha + \beta(L)\,\pi_t + \lambda(L)\,\text{gap}_t + \gamma(L)\,\Delta e_t + \varepsilon_t \tag{6.3}$$

where π_t is the inflation rate, L is the lag operator, gap_t is the output gap, Δe_t is the change in the nominal exchange rate (i.e. depreciation rate), and ε_t is a random error term.[11] All variables are in natural logarithms. An important consideration in this specification is the addition of the exchange rate as a control variable.[12] The exchange rate is important not only for IT in an open economy, but also for emerging economies that are more vulnerable to currency crises. Agénor (2000), for instance, suggests that the exchange rate is affected by interest rate differentials, foreign disturbances and expectations of future exchange rates and risk premiums that depend on domestic factors, such as the size of the domestic public debt and the degree of credibility of the monetary authorities.

The estimation of a single short-run Phillips curve is a suitable approach for the task at hand, since the concept of the sacrifice ratio in this case has a clear meaning.[13] The sacrifice ratio, which is the output gap, required to change inflation by one percentage point is simply the inverse of the coefficient of the gap ($1/\lambda$).[14] This study is focused on the relative magnitude of the ratios since the primary interest is to compare them among different emerging economies. Additionally, in the long run, the sacrifice ratio depends on both the gap and the distribution of the lagged inflation coefficients. Therefore the long relationship is given as follows:

$$\text{Long-run relationship} = \frac{\sum_{i=1}^{n} \lambda_i}{1 - \sum_{i=1}^{n} \beta_i} \tag{6.4}$$

The above equation, Equation 6.4, measures the effect of a one-point increase in the output gap sustained over time by long run or 'steady-state' inflation. The inverse of these ratio measures the increase in the output gap necessary to achieve a 1 per cent reduction of inflation in the long run.

6.3.1.3 Structural estimates of the sacrifice ratio

Cecchetti and Rich (2001) used a structural VAR methodology of decomposing monetary policy into a systematic and a random component to identify changes in the stance of policy.[15] The evaluation of the sacrifice ratio focuses on unanticipated policy evaluation, in which the effects of a contractionary policy correspond to 'pure' (exogenous) monetary tightening rather than a systematic (endogenous) response to other shocks. The specific indicator measures the cumulative output loss after λ periods of a policy shock at time t, where the (persistent) shock is measured as the change in the level of inflation. Using an estimated structural VAR system the dynamic responses of variables to a monetary-policy shock can be traced and an assessment of the quantitative impact of a shift in policy on output and inflation can thereby be allowed.

In this paper the estimation of the sacrifice ratio follows a simple system that includes only output and inflation.[16] This allows a comparison of the results with those obtained from the previous techniques. The structural VAR model proposed to estimate the ratio is as follows:

$$\begin{aligned} \Delta y_t &= \sum_{i=1}^{n} b_{11}^{i}\Delta y_{t-i} + b_{12}^{0}\Delta\pi_t + \sum_{i=1}^{n} b_{12}^{i}\Delta\pi_{t-i} + \varepsilon_t^{y} \\ \Delta\pi_t &= b_{21}^{0}\Delta y_t + \sum_{i=1}^{n} b_{21}^{i}\Delta y_{t-i} + \sum_{i=1}^{n} b_{22}^{i}\Delta\pi_{t-i} + \varepsilon_t^{\pi} \end{aligned} \tag{6.5}$$

where y_t is the aggregate real output in period t and π_t is the rate of inflation from period $t-1$ to t, and the model is shed in terms of rate of changes of these two variables. The innovations, $\varepsilon_t = \left[\varepsilon_t^{y}, \varepsilon_t^{\pi}\right]'$ are assumed to have mean zero, contemporaneous covariance matrix $E\left[\varepsilon_t, \varepsilon_t'\right] = \Omega$ for all t and to be strictly non-autocorrelated. Δ denotes the difference operator $(1 - L)$. Expression 6.5 can be also rewritten more conveniently as:

$$B(L)\begin{bmatrix} \Delta y_t \\ \Delta\pi_t \end{bmatrix} = \begin{bmatrix} \varepsilon_t^{y} \\ \varepsilon_t^{\pi} \end{bmatrix} \tag{6.6}$$

where $B(L)$ is a (2×2) matrix of polynomials in the lag operator. The components of the disturbance (innovation) vector ε_t are identified as shocks to aggregate supply and aggregate demand, respectively.[17] Estimations of the sacrifice ratio are based on the impact over time of structural shocks to output and inflation. To evaluate these magnitudes the impulse responses of the system to structural shocks are calculated. To this end the vector moving average (VMA) representation of Equation 6.5 is used:

$$\begin{bmatrix} \Delta y_t \\ \Delta \pi_t \end{bmatrix} = \begin{bmatrix} \sum_{i=0}^{\infty} a_{11}^i \varepsilon_{t-i}^y + \sum_{i=0}^{\infty} a_{12}^i \varepsilon_{t-i}^{\pi} \\ \sum_{i=0}^{\infty} a_{21}^i \varepsilon_{t-1}^y + \sum_{i=0}^{\infty} a_{22}^i \varepsilon_{t-i}^{\pi} \end{bmatrix} = \begin{bmatrix} A_{11}(L) A_{12}(L) \\ A_{21}(L) A_{22}(L) \end{bmatrix} \begin{bmatrix} \varepsilon_t^y \\ \varepsilon_t^{\pi} \end{bmatrix} \tag{6.7}$$

Specifically, for inflation, the sum of the first λ coefficients in $A_{22}(L)$ measures the effect of a monetary-policy shock on its level λ periods forward. In particular, the effect of a change in ε_t^{π} in period t on the change in inflation λ periods later is a_{22}^{λ}. In the case of output, however, the sacrifice ratio requires consideration of the cumulative effect on its level resulting from a monetary policy shock. This quantity can be expressed as a function of the coefficients in $A_{12}(L)$. An estimate of the sacrifice ratio can then be computed based on the structural impulse response functions from Equation 6.7. Taken together, the relative impact of the monetary policy on output and inflation and hence the sacrifice ratio, over the time horizon λ is just the ratio of these effects and can be calculated as follows:

$$\mathrm{SR}_{\varepsilon^{\pi}}(\lambda) = \frac{\sum_{i=0}^{\lambda} \sum_{j=0}^{i} a_{12}^i}{\sum_{i=0}^{\lambda} a_{22}^i} \tag{6.8}$$

where

$$\mathrm{SR}_{\varepsilon^{\pi}}(\lambda) = \left[\frac{\sum_{j=0}^{\lambda} (\partial y_{t+j} / \partial \varepsilon_t^{\pi})}{(\partial \pi_{t+\lambda} / \partial \varepsilon_t^{\pi})} \right] = \left[\frac{\left(\{\sum_{i=0}^{0} a_{12}^i\} + \{\sum_{i=0}^{1} a_{12}^i\} + \cdots + \{\sum_{i=0}^{\lambda} a_{12}^i\} \right)}{\{\sum_{i=0}^{\lambda} a_{22}^i\}} \right]$$

For a disinflationary monetary strategy undertaken at time t, the numerator measures the cumulative output loss through the first λ periods, while the denominator is the difference in the level of inflation λ periods later. The function SR(λ) is then examined over long periods to study the long-term effects of monetary policy, which can be seen as an advantage of using this approach.

6.3.2 Data

This chapter uses seasonally adjusted quarterly data from 1980 to 2002 on industrial production, consumer prices and nominal exchange rates. The data has been collected from the IMF's International Financial Statistics (IFS) and the corresponding Central Banks and/or National Institutes of Statistics. To conduct this empirical analysis, a sample of 11 emerging economies, divided into two main groups is considered. The first group comprises six emerging economies – Brazil, Chile, Israel, Korea, Mexico and South Africa – that have implemented IT. The second group includes five emerging economies – Nigeria, Philippines, Turkey, Uruguay and Venezuela – with a different monetary policy framework (i.e. monetary targets). These countries were selected in an effort to cover a wide variety of macroeconomic experiences and inflationary histories. They have experienced severe currency pressures that have led either to the abandonment of currency pegs or to large depreciations well beyond what could reasonably have been expected prior to the turbulence (IMF, 1998). The response in terms of monetary policy however has been in all cases to secure macroeconomic stability and to prevent a loss of confidence. They have followed different strategies for disinflation and therefore they have incurred different costs in terms of output. Figures 6.1 and 6.2 present the development of inflation and output in the selected countries during 1981–2002. There is a clear convergence to lower inflation rates for all countries although this seems to be more stable for IT countries.

6.4 Empirical analysis

6.4.1 Empirical results from Ball's approach

Using the first approach the definition of trend inflation was slightly modified. This is estimated as the centred five-quarter moving average of actual inflation instead of the nine-quarter moving

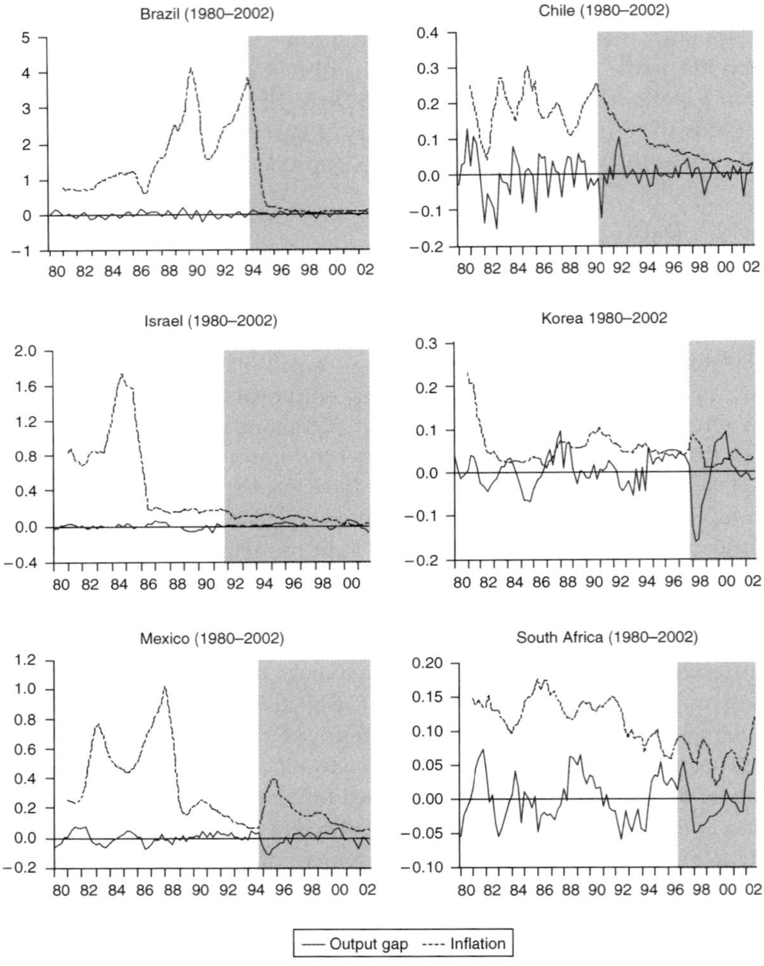

Figure 6.1 Inflation rate and industrial production in IT emerging countries*

* The highlighted area marks the adoption of the IT regime or the date when the countries have implemented important stabilization programmes.

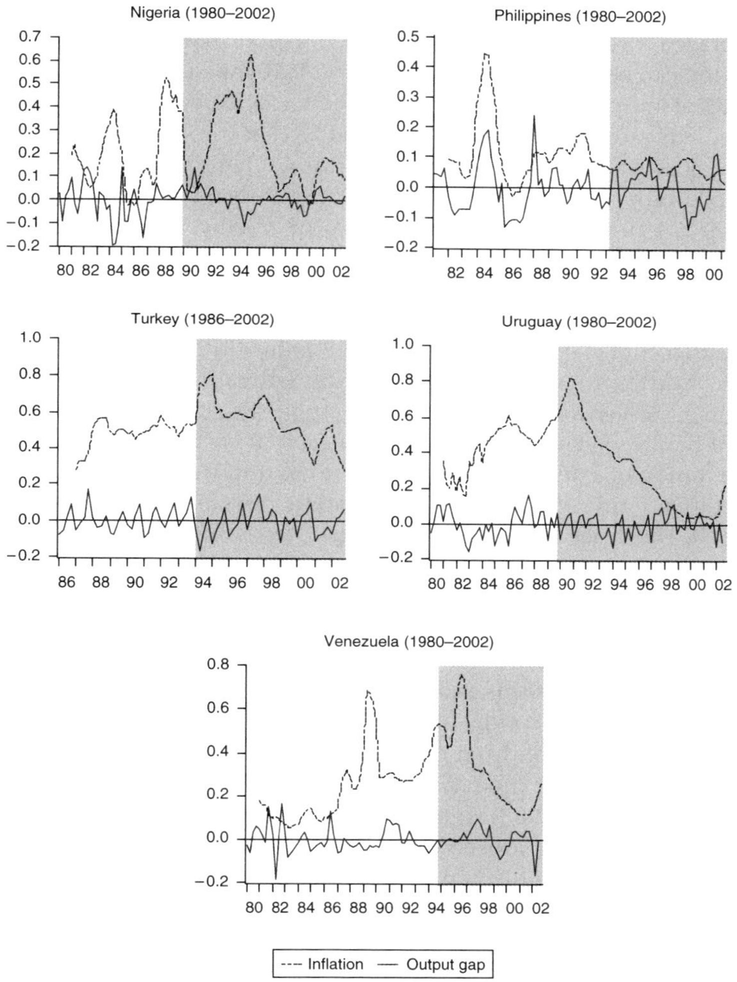

Figure 6.2 Inflation rate and industrial production in non-IT emerging countries*

* The highlighted area marks the adoption of the IT regime or the date when the countries have implemented important stabilization programmes.

average as in Ball (1994). By shortening the range of the moving average procedure a less smoothened inflation trend in which disinflation can be seen more clearly is found.[18] To measure the output gap Ball's assumptions are adopted (see Section 6.3.1.1). Particularly, the output is assumed to be at its potential level at the inflation peak and four quarters after an inflation trough, and it is also assumed that the trend output increases at a constant rate between these two points.[19] Table 6.1 presents the estimations of the sacrifice ratios for all the countries. The results suggest that among the countries with IT, the sacrifice ratio amounted to an average of 2.8, while it was 3.3 per cent for non-IT countries.[20] To be specific, the cost of reducing inflation by one percentage point is on average 2.8 points in terms of output for IT countries, for example. Some of the estimations of the sacrifice ratio, however, are negative. This may suggest that inflation stabilization has been achieved either without output cost or that the implementation of a disinflation programme has not been successful in the medium term achieving stable inflation rates (see Sanchez *et al.*, 1999). The latter is the case, for example, for 12 out of 14 disinflation episodes that present 'after two years' where inflation rates were greater than the ones when these episodes ended.[21]

It is usually presumed that where a disinflationary policy is believed to be credible, and is clearly announced, disinflation will be less costly because firms and households will reset their expectations and reduce them rapidly. This may generate a low sacrifice ratio during the transition from one monetary regime to another. Hence, a negative value for the sacrifice ratio might imply no cost for disinflation. Ball *et al.* (1988) argue that the average level and variability of inflation are crucial aspects for emerging economies along with less independent central banks than for their more advanced counterparts. These aspects can lead to more frequent price and wage adjustments and consequently to a steeper output-inflation trade off. In other words, high inflation reduces the extent of nominal rigidities and thus, the cost of disinflation. It can be argued that for those disinflation episodes that coincide with the implementation of IT, the value of the sacrifice ratio is negative in all the cases. Moreover, the change in inflation and the speed of disinflation have been considerably greater for this group of countries.

To examine in more detail the results presented in Table 6.1, the sample is divided according to the initial level of inflation for the

Table 6.1 Sacrifice ratios during disinflation episodes for emerging economies

Country	Disinflation period	Initial π	Final π	Change in π	Length in quarters	π after 2 years	SR linear trend	Speed of disinflation
With IT								
Brazil	85Q3–86Q4	229.47	137.16	92.31	5	782.4	0.000	18.46
	90Q1–91Q3	3,426.28	474.27	2,952.01	6	1946.18	0.000	492.00
	94Q1–98Q4	2,906.73	2.75	2,903.98	19	6.72	0.000	152.84
Chile	83Q3–84Q3	26.11	20.56	5.55	4	20.25	−0.034	1.39
	85Q3–88Q4	29.53	13.61	15.92	13	25.61	0.008	1.22
	90Q4–99Q4	25.61	3.28	22.33	36	2.99	−0.092	0.62
Korea	90Q4–93Q2	9.56	4.79	4.77	10	4.75	0.023	0.48
	98Q2–99Q3	7.03	0.96	6.07	5	3.84	0.005	1.21
Israel	85Q1–88Q1	406.56	16.85	389.71	12	18.35	−0.001	32.48
	89Q2–90Q3	19.6	17.3	2.3	5	11.88	0.042	0.46
	91Q2–93Q1	18.81	9.93	8.88	7	12.06	0.025	1.27
	94Q4–95Q4	12.55	9.89	2.66	4	7.22	−0.058	0.67
	96Q3-00Q4	11.07	0.84	10.23	17	4.86	−0.062	0.60
Mexico	83Q2–85Q2	100.57	58.23	42.34	8	123.88	0.004	5.29
	87Q4–89Q4	146.42	20.55	125.87	8	19.68	0.001	15.73
	90Q4–94Q2	26.72	7.3	19.42	14	37.9	−0.012	1.39
South Africa	86Q2–88Q3	18.41	12.96	5.45	9	14.35	−0.025	0.61
	91Q4–94Q1	14.54	8.96	5.58	9	6.9	0.084	0.62
	95Q1–96Q1	9.46	6.9	2.56	4	6.77	0.029	0.64
	97Q1–98Q2	8.88	6.86	2.02	5	3.92	0.111	0.40
	98Q4–00Q1	7.54	3.92	3.62	5	6.58	−0.001	0.72
Average		**355.31**	**39.90**	**315.41**	**10**	**146.05**	**0.028**	**34.72**
Without IT								
Philippines	84Q3–86Q4	45.42	−0.72	46.14	9	11.12	0.008	5.13
	91Q2–93Q1	17.59	7.24	10.35	7	7.29	0.007	1.48
	96Q1–97Q2	9.68	6.09	3.59	5	7.46	0.013	0.72
	98Q3–00Q1	9.76	4.27	5.49	5	4.21	0.128	1.10
Nigeria	84Q2–85Q4	38.93	0.4	38.53	6	25.83	0.003	6.42
	88Q4–90Q4	61.14	5.55	55.59	7	51.63	−0.006	7.94
	95Q2–97Q4	73.78	7.03	66.75	10	2.81	−0.003	6.68
	98Q4–99Q4	11.62	2.81	8.81	4	17.41	0.036	2.20
Turkey	88Q3–90Q3	71.11	60.83	10.28	8	68.49	0.025	1.29
	92Q1–92Q4	70.29	65.28	5.01	3	109.85	0.004	1.67
	94Q4–96Q4	109.85	79.48	30.37	8	75.02	0.004	3.80
	98Q1–01Q1	91.44	48.3	43.14	12	51.18	−0.003	3.60
Uruguay	86Q2–88Q1	76.95	60.01	16.94	7	95.45	−0.040	2.42
	90Q4–01Q1	117.09	4.39	112.7	37	7.66	−0.022	3.05
Venezuela	84Q4–85Q4	13.22	10.17	3.05	4	31.07	0.099	0.76
	89Q3–92Q2	80.99	31.52	49.47	11	56.72	−0.011	4.50
	96Q3–01Q2	95.21	12.87	82.34	19	20.26	−0.017	4.33
Average		**58.47**	**23.85**	**34.62**	**10**	**37.85**	**0.036**	3.36

* The average sacrifice ratio is calculated just for positive values.

different episodes of disinflation. Following the classification in Bruno and Easterly (1998), four groups are considered: (1) the first group comprises countries with initial levels of inflation equal or more than 40 per cent, (2) the second group includes countries with initial levels of inflation between 20 and 40 per cent, (3) the third group has rates of inflation between 10 and 20 per cent and (4) the last one comprises countries with less than 10 per cent. In general, the higher the initial level of inflation, the lower the sacrifice ratio. A scatter graph is given in Figure 6.3 for the whole sample. According to Figure 6.3 there is a clear negative association between the variables.[22] More variability is observed in IT countries presenting lower values of the sacrifice ratio in all the cases. Finally, most of the disinflation episodes considered in the group with higher initial levels of inflation belong to countries that have not implemented IT. More disinflation episodes with moderate and low initial levels of inflation pertain to countries, which have adopted this regime.

Similar conclusions are observed when the results are divided according to the 1980s and the 1990s. During the 1980s, the sacrifice ratio, the initial inflation, the change in inflation and the speed of disinflation were greater in IT countries than in non-IT countries. This tendency, however, was the reverse for all the indicators in the 1990s.[23] Moreover, there is some evidence of a reduction in the sacrifice ratios for both country groups, although these reductions tend to be greater in those countries that have adopted explicit inflation targets. Overall, the results obtained from this first approach

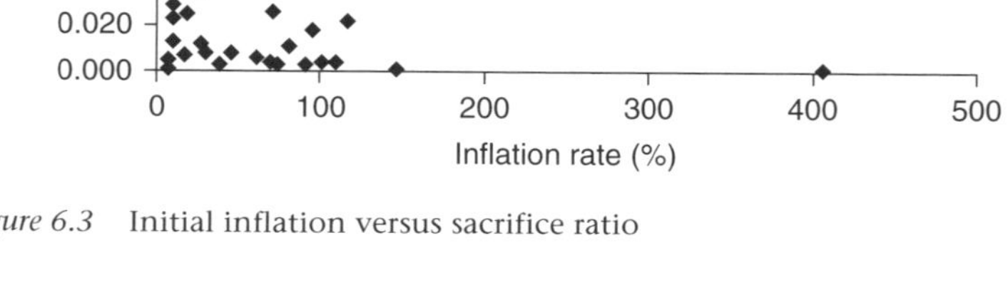

Figure 6.3 Initial inflation versus sacrifice ratio

reflect the effectiveness of the measures implemented under the IT regime and the convergence to stable and low values of inflation with a lower cost in terms of output than the rest of the countries.

6.4.2 Econometric results derived from the Phillips curve

This section reports the estimation of sacrifice ratios estimating the supply slope coefficients from Equation 6.3 using an ordinary least squares (OLS). Two periods are considered for each country: the pre-reform and the post-reform period. The date selected for the division corresponds to the implementation of IT for the first group of countries and to the date where crucial stabilization programmes or institutional reforms took place in countries belonging to the second group (see Table 6.2). Regressions are computed for each country, including eight lags of inflation and four lags of the output gap and the depreciation rate. Subsequently, those variables that are insignificant at the 10 per cent level using the general to specific modelling approach are omitted (see Charemza and Deadman, 1997). Dummies and other variables such as changes in oil prices are included, when necessary, to improve the estimation.[24] The final parsimonious models are then used to estimate the sacrifice ratios.

The estimation of Equation 6.3 implies that the variables included in the specification are expected to be stationary, *I(0)*.[25] The

Table 6.2 Date of the reform period division

Country	Date
With IT	
Israel	1992q1
South Africa	1997q1
Brazil	1994q3
Chile	1991q1
Mexico	1995q1
Korea	1998q1
Without IT	
Nigeria	1990q1
Philippines	1993q3
Turkey	1995q3
Uruguay	1990q1
Venezuela	1989q1

augmented Dickey–Fuller (ADF) and the Phillips–Perron (PP) test for unit roots are performed for the variables included in the model. The number of lags is selected according to the Akaike (AIC) and Schwarz (SIC) criterion. The results suggest that the variables are $I(0)$.[26] Equation 6.3 is estimated for each country. In general, the models fit the data reasonably well and the diagnostic test statistics suggest that the residuals have satisfactory statistical properties.[27] Tables 6.3 and 6.4

Table 6.3 Sacrifice ratios from the estimation of Phillips curves (short-run)

Country	Pre-reform period	Post-reform period
With IT		
Mexico	3.92*	10.38*
	(1.64)	(1.72)
South Africa	17.27*	3.33**
	(1.65)	(4.27)
Israel	1.64**	6.59*
	(3.70)	(1.74)
Korea	−19.61*	−6.21**
	(−1.77)	(−3.08)
Chile	2.81**	−26.08
	(4.61)	(−1.21)
Brazil	0.93***	26.15*
	(5.13)	(1.45)
Average	**5.31**	**11.61**
Without IT		
Philippines	5.08**	13.23**
	(4.31)	(3.32)
Nigeria	3.62**	−1.55**
	(2.98)	(−3.03)
Turkey	−3.55**	6.76
	(−2.80)	(1.30)
Uruguay	−3.13**	17.9*
	(−3.20)	(1.61)
Venezuela	−15.62	6.67**
	(−0.95)	(2.60)
Average	**4.35**	**12.60**

The overall average of the sacrifice ratio is computed just for positive values. *t*-statistic in parenthesis is computed according to Hendry (1989), pp. 51–53.

*, **, *** denotes 1%, 5% and 10% level of significance, respectively.

Table 6.4 Sacrifice ratios from the estimation of Phillips curves (long-run)

Country	Pre-reform period	Post-reform period
With IT		
Mexico	−1.11	1.58**
	(−1.40)	(3.40)
South Africa	−0.05	4.12**
	(−0.06)	(4.12)
Israel	1.23**	1.65*
	(4.01)	(1.64)
Korea	−3.55*	−5.66**
	(−1.64)	(−3.44)
Chile	0.53**	−4.19
	(2.91)	(−1.13)
Brazil	0.29***	7.54
	(8.16)	(1.45)
Average	**0.68**	**2.45**
Without IT		
Philippines	1.94**	4.77
	(4.56)	(1.50)
Nigeria	−0.75**	−0.25**
	(−2.03)	(−5.57)
Turkey	−4.57**	1.43
	(2.07)	(1.32)
Uruguay	−0.49**	1.84
	(2.74)	(1.55)
Venezuela	−3.41	0.32
	(−0.92)	(0.91)
Average	**1.94**	**2.18**

The overall average of the sacrifice ratio is computed just for positive values. *t*-statistic in parenthesis is computed according to Hendry (1989), pp. 51–53.
*, **, *** denotes 1%, 5% and 10% level of significance, respectively.

present the values of the implied sacrifice ratios in the short and the long run, respectively, for all countries in the pre- and post-reform periods. Due to space constraints the results of the Unit Root tests are not presented here, but are available on request.

According to the Phillips curve theory the expected value for λ should be positive. However, recent evidence suggests that an attempt to stabilize high inflation is not necessarily contractionary, and it may be expansionary. Bruno and Easterly (1998), for example, examine the case of 26 countries that have had episodes of high inflation over the period 1961–92.[28] They show that per capita growth is negative during high inflation crises, but after stabilization growth recovers strongly. This contradicts the view that low rates of inflation are associated with lower growth in the short- to medium-term. Similarly, Mendoza (1998) suggests that after the devaluation of the peso in Mexico in 1995, the increase in inflation induced a contraction of the economy.

The results presented in Tables 6.3 and 6.4 are mixed. Taking into consideration the short-run average estimates (see Table 6.3) the results suggest that IT countries have higher sacrifice ratio during the post-reform period rather than during the pre-reform period. Chile and Korea, however, appear to have negative values, although for the case of Chile this is not statistically significant. For the second group, similar conclusions can be derived. All countries increased the value of the sacrifice ratio in the post-reform period with the exception of Nigeria. Interestingly, the average values for both country groups are very similar. Nevertheless, if Brazil is not included in the first group, the increase in the sacrifice ratio is less for IT countries.[29] More specifically, the sacrifice ratios for IT countries and non-IT countries are 6.77 and 12.60, respectively. Another interesting observation is that the sign of the sacrifice ratio is the same before and after the reform for six countries – Brazil, Israel, Korea, Mexico, Nigeria, South Africa – five of them belonging to the first group.

The long-run estimations of the sacrifice ratio are presented in Table 6.4. The pattern followed by both country groups is very similar to the one just mentioned even though the value of the sacrifice ratio is considerably smaller. Only the estimated coefficients of Israel, Brazil, Korea, Philippines and Nigeria carry the same sign over the two sample periods. Generally, countries with IT have raised the value of the sacrifice ratio from 0.68 to 2.45 whereas the non-IT countries have increased it from 1.94 to 2.18.[30] In the long run, the cost of reducing inflation has become greater in IT countries. This finding may reflect the achievement of stable rates of inflation in these countries supporting previous findings regarding the initial level of inflation-sacrifice ratio nexus (see Section 6.4.1).

Table 6.5 Chow stability test

Country	F-Statistic	Probability
With IT		
Mexico (94q1)	3.40	0.001
Brazil (94q2)	20.40	0.000
Chile (90q4)	7.09	0.000
Israel (91q4)	2.51	0.007
Korea (97q4)	2.25	0.026
South Africa (96q4)	3.61	0.001
Without IT		
Nigeria (89q4)	−0.39	0.973
Philippines (93q2)	4.94	0.000
Turkey (95q2)	1.31	0.253
Uruguay (89q4)	0.34	0.991
Venezuela (88q4)	−0.21	0.999

Ho: Regressions are the same or there is structural stability.
F-stat = [RSSes − (RSSsl + RSSs2)/k]/[(RSSsl + RSSs2)/($n1 + n2 - 2k$)].

To check for parameter stability the Chow-test is applied for each country over the full sample period.[31] The results are presented in Table 6.5. The null hypothesis of unchanged parameters or stability test is rejected at the 5 per cent level in all IT countries and Philippines. This may suggest that the adoption of IT has contributed to changes in the economic structure of these countries.[32] Additionally, the estimations of the Phillips curve are used to generate out-of-sample forecasts from the period of policy shift to the end of the sample period in the case of IT countries. Figure 6.4 shows the forecasting results. In IT countries, apart from Mexico, actual inflation is generally below the forecast inflation. Table 6.6 reports the root mean squared (RMS), the mean absolute error (MAE) and the Theil inequality (TI) coefficient from forecasting inflation. For the first two forecast error statistics it can be said that the smaller the error, the better the forecast. The coefficient derived from the third statistic always lies between zero and one, where zero indicates a perfect fit. The statistics suggest a satisfactory forecasts for IT countries. To summarize, there is no clear evidence of a possible shift in the output–inflation trade off after the implementation of IT.

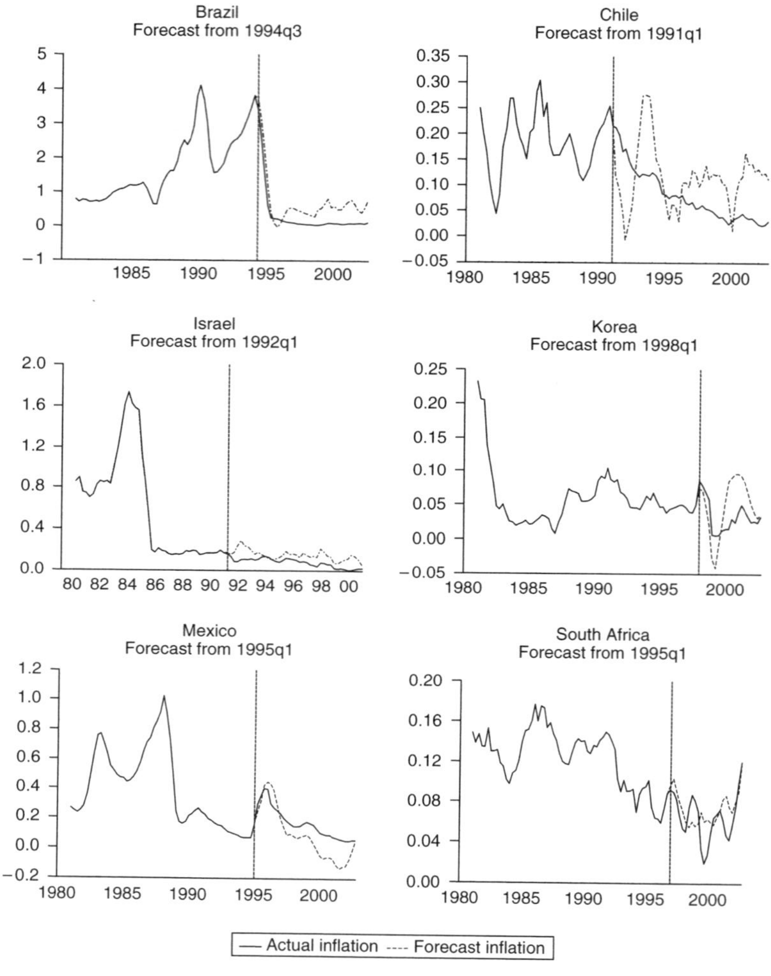

Figure 6.4 Inflation forecasts in IT countries*

* The vertical line represents the onset of forecasting and the dashed line is the forecast of inflation.

Table 6.6 Forecast evaluation of inflation

Country	RMSE	MAE	TIC	*T*
With IT				
Israel	0.062	0.048	0.055	40
South Africa	0.016	0.013	0.075	24
Brazil	0.302	0.216	0.086	34
Chile	0.066	0.047	0.221	48
Mexico	0.076	0.057	0.095	32
Korea	0.02	0.016	0.211	20

* *T* represents the number of out-of-sample observations.

6.4.3 Identification and estimation of the structural VAR model

To obtain the structural impulse response functions (SIR), the reduced-form VAR representation of Equation 6.5 in conjunction with identifying restrictions are used. The unrestricted VAR representation is given by:

$$y_t - D_1 y_{t-1} - D_2 y_{t-2} - \cdots - D_k y_{t-k} = D(L) y_t = \mu_t \qquad (6.9)$$

where y_t is an $(n \times 1)$ vector of endogenous variables, $D(L)$ is a kth-order lag polynomial matrix, and μ_t is the $(n \times 1)$ vector of innovations to the system. It is assumed that μ_t has zero mean and is serially uncorrelated with the covariance matrix $E[\mu_t \mu_t] = \Sigma$ for all t. Equation 6.9 can be estimated and inverted to yield its unrestricted VMA representation:[33]

$$y_t = \mu_t + C_1 \mu_{t-1} + C_2 \mu_{t-2} + \cdots = C(L) \mu_t \qquad (6.10)$$

From Equations 6.6 and 6.7, the VAR and VMA representations of the structural system can be written, respectively, as:

$$B_0 y_t = B_1 y_{t-1} + B_2 y_{t-2} + \cdots + B_k y_{t-k} + \varepsilon_t \qquad (6.11)$$

and

$$y_t = A_0 \varepsilon_t + A_1 \varepsilon_{t-1} + \cdots = A(L) \varepsilon_t \qquad (6.12)$$

Equations 6.11 and 6.12 imply that:

$$E[(A_0\varepsilon_t)(A_0\varepsilon_t)'] = A_0\Omega A'_{00} = \Sigma = E[(\mu_t)(\mu'_t)] \tag{6.13}$$

and

$$A(L) = C(L)A_0 \tag{6.14}$$

The estimation of the matrix A_0 becomes crucial to link the unrestricted VAR to the structural VAR model. Complete identification for A_0 requires a total of n^2 restrictions. One set of identifying restrictions is based on the assumption that the structural shocks are uncorrelated and have unit variance. That is, assuming that $\Omega = I_n$, where I_n is the $(n \times n)$ identity matrix, $A_0 A'_0 = \Sigma$, where Σ is an estimable matrix with three free parameters. Finally, since A_0 is 2×2 one more restriction is needed to secure identification. Following Blanchard and Quah (1989), the additional restriction for Cecchetti's model is that aggregate demand shocks have no permanent effect on the level of output. This is equivalent to the condition that

$$A_{12}(1) = \sum_{i=0}^{\infty} a_{12}^{i} = 0.$$

Once A_0 is estimated, the SIF are generated in order to obtain the response of the level of output and inflation at each horizon to the monetary shock. Dividing the appropriate quantities at each horizon provides the sacrifice ratio (see Equation 6.8). Cecchetti's model identifies two shocks and associates shifts in monetary policy with aggregate demand disturbance.[34] This scheme provides a good approximation for analysing the relative importance of nominal and real shocks and therefore for the estimation of the sacrifice ratio. In the interest of simplicity, this chapter is restricted to the analysis of Cecchetti's two-equation model to compare the relative magnitude of the sacrifice ratios under alternative techniques. The inclusion of more variables would be interesting for future research although there is evidence that the estimates from structural VAR models are very imprecise.

Stationary properties of the series are examined to determine the degree of integration and the presence of cointegrating relationships.

The results from the application of the Dickey–Fuller test provided evidence that output (in logs) and inflation contain a unit root.[35] According to Cecchetti and Rich (2001) these findings are primarily important for the concept of a sacrifice ratio. The evidence of a unit root in the output process allows long-run restriction on the effects of aggregate demand shocks to be well defined and meaningful, while the evidence of a unit root in the inflation process allows for permanent shifts in its level. The lag-length of the reduced-form VAR varies from each country according to the Akaike Information and Schwarz criterion. Table 6.7 presents the point estimates of the sacrifice ratio at horizons of one to five years for the two country groups. The results should be interpreted as the cumulative output loss corresponding to a permanent one-percentage-point decline in the rate of inflation measured on an annual basis. A negative value for the sacrifice ratio might imply no cost for disinflation.

Overall, the results for the estimation of the sacrifice ratios suggest relatively constant values as the horizon grows for all countries. Exceptions are South Africa and Philippines where the highest value is reached after three years and starts to decrease thereafter. Observing

Table 6.7 Sacrifice ratio estimates for emerging economies

Country	*n*				
	4	8	12	16	20
With IT					
Brazil	−0.044	−0.022	−0.019	−0.021	−0.022
Chile	−0.269	−0.181	−0.047	−0.229	−0.103
Israel	−0.015	−0.083	−0.205	−0.246	−0.294
Korea	0.378	0.409	0.353	0.361	0.361
Mexico	0.364	0.515	0.351	0.433	0.381
South Africa	1.498	0.485	2.024	0.757	1.479
Average	**0.32**	**0.19**	**0.41**	**0.18**	**0.30**
Without IT					
Nigeria	0.099	0.074	0.657	0.257	0.499
Philippines	3.432	6.873	10.477	7.061	5.711
Turkey	−0.219	−0.170	−0.142	−0.122	−0.110
Uruguay	0.057	0.111	0.109	0.114	0.114
Venezuela	0.069	0.055	0.057	0.057	0.056
Average	**0.69**	**1.39**	**2.23**	**1.47**	**1.25**

the average values, it is clear that the sacrifice ratios are higher in non-IT countries. Due to the particular characteristics of the emerging economies considered in this study, we re-estimate the model including dummy variables for known periods of crisis or policy reforms (see Table 6.2). Particular attention is paid to those countries with negative values for the sacrifice ratio. The results in general do not present significant changes. The only exception is Israel in which the values of the sacrifice ratio become positive even though near to zero. These results are not presented here in detail, but are available on request.

Additionally, estimations of the sacrifice ratio are carried out for the post-reform periods. The results at different horizons are presented in Table 6.8. The sacrifice ratio estimations are relatively constant as the horizon grows. This pattern is supported by the results found by Cecchetti and Rich (2001) for the US sacrifice ratio using the same approach. Generally, there is a decrease in the estimations for the non-IT countries, but on average the estimated values are higher than those obtained for IT countries. Regarding the first country group, Chile and Korea are the countries with highest values

Table 6.8 Sacrifice ratio estimates for emerging economies in the post-reform period

Country	*n*				
	4	**8**	**12**	**16**	**20**
With IT					
Brazil	0.003	0.006	0.008	0.009	0.011
Chile	0.405	0.436	0.439	0.438	0.438
Israel	−0.312	−0.284	−0.278	−0.285	−0.242
Korea	1.041	1.946	1.530	1.683	1.669
Mexico	0.051	0.033	0.030	0.031	0.031
South Africa	−0.118	−0.118	−0.118	−0.118	−0.118
Average	**0.18**	**0.34**	**0.27**	**0.29**	**0.30**
Without IT					
Nigeria	0.015	0.022	0.024	0.024	0.025
Philippines	1.323	0.958	0.800	0.799	0.777
Turkey	−0.050	−0.035	−0.023	−0.013	−0.006
Uruguay	0.746	0.825	0.846	0.854	0.858
Venezuela	0.212	0.116	0.133	0.145	0.142
Average	**0.45**	**0.38**	**0.36**	**0.36**	**0.36**

of the sacrifice ratio, but also the ones with lower and more stable rates of inflation. This supports the view that the lower the initial rates of inflation the higher the sacrifice ratios are expected to be due to nominal rigidities. Overall, the results indicate that in countries where the process of disinflation has been accompanied by the adoption of explicit inflation targets, sacrifice ratios have increased less (or even declined over time) than non-IT countries. Furthermore, these countries have achieved lower and more stable levels of inflation.

6.5 Conclusions

This study carries out estimations for the sacrifice ratio of 11 emerging economies using three different approaches: (1) comparison of actual changes in inflation with changes in standard measures of output, (2) estimation of aggregate supply curves and (3) employment of a structural VAR model. This allows sacrifice ratios to be estimated and compared, overcoming any possible shortcomings of each approach. Using the first approach it was found that for the countries with IT, the sacrifice ratio amounted to an average of 2.8 while the equivalent average is 3.3 per cent for non-IT countries. Moreover, the changes in inflation and the speed of disinflation have been considerably higher for IT countries. Some evidence that lower initial rates of inflation are associated with higher sacrifice ratios was also found. During the 1980s the sacrifice ratio, the initial inflation, the change in inflation and the speed of disinflation were higher in IT. However, this was not supported during the 1990s. Additionally, a reduction in the sacrifice ratios for both country groups is observed, even though the reduction tends to be higher for IT countries.

Interesting findings are also obtained from the estimation of the Phillips curve. The coefficients for the sacrifice ratio in the short-run are in average quite similar in the pre-reform period for both country groups (the average is computed for positive values of the sacrifice ratio). Generally, negative values of the sacrifice ratio are mainly observed in non-IT countries. However, this is also supported for Korea. Similar conclusion can be drawn from the post-reform period. Negatives values may be explained by substantial supply shocks or the implementation of unsuccessful stabilization programmes. In the long run the values of the sacrifice ratios are considerably smaller. The cost of reducing inflation, however, seems to be higher in IT countries. Moreover, using the final approach the estimations of the sacrifice ratios suggest relatively constant values as the horizon grows for all countries. It was found that non-IT countries have higher values of the sacrifice ratio. When the model is estimated for the post-reform periods, however, the results suggest a general decrease in the values of the sacrifice ratio for the non-IT countries. Considering IT countries, Chile and Korea have the highest values of the sacrifice ratio. Generally, the results may suggest that lower initial rates of inflation are associated with higher sacrifice ratios.

In conclusion, the empirical evidence of this study suggests that emerging economies with IT have a better ability to achieve low and stable levels of inflation. However, this policy regime may be accompanied by other important structural and institutional developments, which are not considered in this chapter; this could be an issue for further research.

Notes

I am indebted to Miguel Angel Mendoza and Robert W. Rich for encouraging me to continue working on this topic and for their helpful comments. I also thank Wojciech Charemza, Panicos Demetriades, Anthony Garratt, Monica Hernandez, Ali al-Nowaihi, Julio Santaella, George Saridakis, Alberto Torres, and seminar participants at the University of Leicester, Bank of Mexico, the 7th International Conference in Macroeconomics and Finance and the International Conference on Emerging Markets and Global Risk Management for their valuable comments and discussions. Financial support from the National Council of Science and Technology (CONACYT) in Mexico is gratefully acknowledged. Any remaining errors are mine.

1. According to a survey carried out by Fry *et al.*, 2000; between 1990 and 1998, the percentage of economies with inflation targets increased over tenfold, from 5 to 58 per cent of the sample. The analysis was based on data provided by 93 central banks that responded to the Bank of England questionnaire.
2. Countries such as Brazil in 1999, Israel in 1991 and Mexico in 1994.
3. This may not be the case for industrialized countries where disinflation had largely been completed by the time of the IT adoption.
4. Lee's (1999) findings are based on the comparison between three IT countries (New Zealand, Canada, the United Kingdom) and three non- IT countries (Australia, the United States of America, Germany).
5. The empirical analysis was conducted for the 1980–99 period introducing three country groups. The first one includes countries that have had IT in place until 1995. The second one is composed of five emerging economies

on their way to IT during the 1990s. The last one is composed of ten industrial economy countries that are not inflation targeters.

6. Mayes and Chapple (1995) discuss in detail possible shortcomings using sacrifice ratios.
7. Ball (1994) examined all OECD countries for which trend inflation has stayed below 20 per cent since 1960. He concludes that the sacrifice ratio is lower when disinflation is quick and when w^{a}ge setting is more flexible.
8. However, a shortcoming of this method is that only shifts in demand affect inflation. There are no supply shocks.
9. Phillips (1958) describes the relationship between wage inflation and unemployment, where there is a trade off between unemployment deviations from its equilibrium value and wage inflation. For a more detailed discussion of the historical development of the Phillips curve see Ball *et al.* (1988), Mankiw (2001) and Razzak (2002).
10. The output gap's relationship to inflation can be simplified by setting supply shocks to zero and abstracting from the determinants of inflation expectations. This leads to a Phillips curve equation that yields a relationship between unexpected inflation changes and the output gap, $\pi_t = \pi_t^* + \lambda(y_t - y_t^*)$. Nonetheless, there are many factors to be considered when determining short-run inflation behaviour (e.g. the speed of adjustment of inflation expectations, the size and persistence of supply shocks, the long and variable lags of monetary policy).
11. Industrial production (IP) is used as an approximation of the output cost of inflation stabilization due to the availability of the data under the study period. The estimated series are an approximation of the output gap between actual and potential output. The latter is calculated with a Hodrick–Prescott filter with a 1,600 penalty parameter (recommended for quarterly data). The output gap variable is then measured as the logarithmic deviation of the output (IP) from the trend. The unemployment gap can be also used as a proxy of excess demand pressures. The limitation of the data, however, does not allow us to experiment with the latter.
12. It can be also argued that the (growth rate of) real import prices may be used as an alternative control variable for supply shocks. However, we do not have data available for all countries under the study period.
13. The advantage of this approach is that information on disinflationary episodes and also periods characterized by rising inflation are both taken into account. Moreover, an effort is made to control for a variety of factors other than aggregate demand shifts that may influence the short-term behaviour of output and inflation. A shortcoming, however, is that the estimated sacrifice ratio is not varying over time.
14. For example, if the model is estimated using quarterly data, with inflation measured at annual rates, then $4 \times \lambda$ should be substituted for the parameter if what we want to estimate is the percentage of a year's output loss in reducing inflation by one percentage point (see Cozier and Wilkinson, 1991).

15. A structural VAR can be viewed as a dynamic simultaneous-equations model with identifying restrictions based on economic theory. Specifically, the structural VAR relates the observed movements in a variable to a set of structural shocks – innovations that are fundamental in the sense that they can provide an economic interpretation.
16. Cecchetti and Rich (2001) examined two other VAR models, a three-equation model of Shapiro and Watson (1988), which adds an equation in real interest rates and a four-equation model by Gali (1992). They suggest that the sacrifice ratios obtained from structural VAR models are highly sensitive to the size of the model and the identification restrictions imposed. Our analysis is restricted to the two-equation model in the interest of simplicity.
17. There is an assumption concerning the use of the aggregate demand (AD) shock as a proxy for a monetary policy shock. Specifically, the assumption is either that the only source of AD shocks is monetary policy, or that the economy responds to monetary policy in the same way that it does to other demand shocks.
18. When the nine-period centred moving average of actual inflation is used as the trend inflation, the number of episodes is lower for most of the countries.
19. There are no significant differences in the estimation of the output gap if the standard Hodrick–Prescott–Filter approach is used.
20. This average is computed just for positive values of the sacrifice ratio.
21. Another issue to be considered is that during the crisis periods while output is in a downward trend, high levels of inflation rates are observed. Hence, a relative rise in output is very likely to occur in line with a fall in inflation in the post-crisis period. This is the case for countries such as Venezuela (89Q3–92Q2) and Mexico (90Q4–94Q2).
22. Similar conclusions can be drawn from other studies such as Andersen and Wascher (1999), Sanchez *et al.* (1999) and Laubach and Posen (1997).
23. These results may support those found by Lee (1999) for industrialized economies in the sense that a disinflation environment is observed during the 1990s. However, in the case of emerging economies we found evidence that IT may contribute to lower and stable levels of inflation.
24. Dummies capture important changes in the structure of the economy for each country. More details are available on request.
25. The output gap is by definition stationary and the annual change in the nominal exchange rate is expected to be $I(0)$ as well.
26. Brazil is the only country where inflation presents weak evidence of stationarity. It should be mentioned that the series for inflation are smoothed using a five-quarter moving average of actual inflation before testing for Unit Roots.
27. Standard errors are corrected for robustness when required with the Newey–West HAC method.
28. An episode of high inflation is defined as a period of two years or more in which inflation exceeds 40 per cent annually.

29. Brazil experienced annual rates of inflation above 2,500 per cent at the beginning of the 1990s.
30. Nevertheless for the latter group only Philippines has a positive value for the sacrifice ratio in the pre-reform period.
31. The optimal specification is obtained through the general to specific method outlined earlier.
32. Three more stability tests are carried out: Recursive residuals test, Cusum test and Cusum of squares test. According to these tests, there is some evidence of parameter instability mainly for IT countries. In non-IT countries, with the exception of Turkey there is some indication of a structural break but the results are not supported with the *F*-test.
33. Detailed analysis of this procedure can be found in Greene (2003), 597–600.
34. The restrictions in the Cecchetti's model, however, fail to identify separate components of the aggregate demand disturbance. In other words, the estimated monetary-policy shock would include not only policy shifts, but also other shocks such as those related to government spending or investment functions.
35. Output is measured by the Industrial Production index (IPI) and inflation is measured by the Consumer Price index (CPI). Output growth is measured as 100 times the difference in the log-level of the output series while inflation rate is measured as 400 times the difference in the log-levels of the price series. In order to have a stationary series, the inflation rate is differenced again, and then both series are de-meaned for the VAR estimation. It should be mentioned that in the Philips curve section we claim that inflation is *I*(0). This is due to the fact that inflation was smoothed using a five-quarter moving average of actual inflation before testing for Unit Roots. To avoid this disparity, it can be argued that the Phillips curve estimation may be obtained by using inflation in first differences.

References

Agénor, P.-R. (2000), 'Monetary policy under flexible exchange rates: an introduction to inflation targeting', *The World Bank*, Washington, DC.

Andersen, P. (1992), 'OECD country experiences with disinflation', in: *Inflation, Disinflation and Monetary Policy*, Sydney: Reserve Bank of Australia, pp. 104–73.

Andersen, P. S. and W. L. Wascher (1999), 'Sacrifice ratios and the conduct of monetary policy in conditions of low inflation', *BIS Working Papers* No. 82.

Ball, Laurence (1994), 'What determines the Sacrifice Ratio', *NBER Working Paper* No. w4306.

Ball, L., G. Mankiw and D. Romer (1988), 'The new Keynesian economics and the output-inflation trade-off', *Brooking Papers on Economic Activity*, 1, 1–65.

Bernanke B. and F. Mishkin (1997), 'Inflation targeting: a new framework for monetary policy?', *The Journal of Economic Perspectives*, 11(2), 97–116.

Bernanke B., T. Laubach, F. Mishkin and A. Posen (1999), *Inflation Targeting: Lessons from International Experience*, Princeton University Press: Princeton, NJ.

Blanchard, O. J. (1984), 'The Lucas critique and the Volcker deflation', *American Economy Review*, 74(2), 211–15.

Blanchard, O. J. and D. Quah (1989), 'The dynamic effects of aggregate demand and supply disturbances', *American Economic Review*, 79, 655–73.

Bogdanski, J., A. Tombini and S. Ribeiro C. Werlang (2000), 'Implementing inflation targeting in Brazil', *Bank of Brazil*, Working Papers, July.

Bruno, M. and W. Easterly (1998), 'Inflation crises and long-run growth', *Journal of Monetary Economics*, 41, 3–26.

Cecchetti, S. and R. Rich (2001), 'Structural estimates of the U.S. sacrifice ratio', *Journal of Business and Economics Statistics*, 19(4), 416–27.

Charemza, W. and D. Deadman (1997), *New Directions in Econometric Practice: General to Specific Modelling, Cointegration and Vector Autoregression*, 2nd edn, Edward Elgar.

Corbo, V., O. Landerretche and K. Schmidt-Hebbel (2002), 'Objetivos de inflación en América Latina', *Gaceta de Economía*, ITAM, Numero especial.

Corbo, V., O. Landerretche and K. Schmidt-Hebbel (2001), 'Assessing inflation targeting after a decade of world experience', *International Journal of Finance and Economics*, 6(4), 343–68.

Cozier, B. and G. Wilkinson (1991), 'Some evidence on hysteresis and the costs of disinflation in Canada', *Bank of Canada*, Technical Report No. 55.

Debelle, G. (1997), 'Inflation targeting in practice', *IMF Working Papers* 97/35, International Monetary Fund.

Debelle, G., P. Masson, M. Savastano and S. Sharma (1998), 'Inflation targeting as a framework for monetary policy', *Economic Issues* No.15, IMF, September.

Filardo, A. (1998), 'New evidence on the output cost of fighting inflation', Federal Reserve Bank of Kansas City, *Economic Review*, 3rd quarter.

Fraga, Arminio, Ilan Goldfajn and André Minilla (2003), 'Inflation targeting in emerging market economies', Paper presented at the *NBER* Macroeconomics Annual Conference.

Fry, M., D. Julius, L. Mahadeva, S. Roger and G. Sterne (2000), 'Key issues in the choice of monetary policy framework', in Mahadeva L. and Sterne G. (eds), *Monetary Frameworks in a Global Context*, Routledge, London.

Gali, J. (1992), 'How well does the IS-LM model fit postwar U.S. data?', *Quarterly Journal of Economics*, 107, 709–38.

Groeneveld, J., K. Koedijk and C. Kool (1998), 'Inflation dynamics and monetary strategies: evidence from six industrialized countries', *Open Economies Review*, 9, 21–38.

Haldane, A. (ed.) (1995), *Targeting Inflation*, Bank of England, London.

Honda, Y. (2000), 'Some tests on the effects of inflation targeting in New Zealand, Canada, and the UK', *Economics Letters*, 66, 1–6

Hutchison, M. M. and C. E. Walsh (1998), 'The output-inflation tradeoff and Central Bank Reform: evidence from New Zealand', *The Economic Journal*, 108 (May), 703–25.

Kuttner, K. and A. Posen (1999), 'Does talk matter after all? Inflation targeting and Central Bank behaviour', *Federal Reserve Bank of New York*, Staff Report No. 88 (October).

Laubach, T. and A. Posen (1997), 'Some comparative evidence on the effectiveness of inflation targeting', *Federal Reserve Bank of New York*, Research Paper No. 9714, April.

Lee, J. (1999), 'Inflation targeting in practice: further evidence', *Contemporary Economic Policy*, 17(3), 332–47.

Leiderman, L. and G. Bufman (2000), 'Inflation targeting under a crawling band exchange rate regime: lessons from Israel', in M. I. Blejer, A. Ize, A. M. Leone, and S. Werlang (eds), *Inflation Targeting in Practice: Strategic and Operational Issues and Application to Emerging Market Economies*, International Monetary Fund, Washington, DC.

Masson, P. R., M. A. Savastano and S. Sharma (1997), 'The scope for inflation targeting in developing countries', *IMF Working Paper* 97/130.

Mankiw, G. (2001), 'The inexorable and mysterious trade-off between inflation and unemployment', *The Economic Journal*, 111(471), 45–61.

Mayes, D. and B. Chapple (1995), 'The cost and benefits of disinflation: a critique of the sacrifice ratio', *Reserve Bank of New Zealand Bulletin,* 58(1), 9–21.

McCallum, B. (1996), 'Inflation targeting in Canada, New Zealand, Sweden, the United Kingdom, and in general', *NBER Working Paper* 5579.

Mendoza, M. A. (1998), 'Inflacion y Crecimiento Económico en México', *Monetaria*, XXI–(21), abril–junio.

Mishkin, F. (1997), 'Strategies from controlling inflation', in *Monetary Policy and Inflation Targeting: Proceedings of a Conference*, Economic Group, Reserve Bank of Australia, pp. 7–38.

Mishkin, F. and A. Posen (1997), 'Inflation targeting: lessons from four countries', Federal Reserve Bank of New York, *Economic Policy Review,* 3, 9–110.

Mishkin, F. and K. Schmidt-Hebbel (2002), 'A decade of inflation targeting in the world: what do we known and what do we need to know', in N. Loaza, and R. Soto (eds), *Inflation Targeting: Design, Performance,* Challenges, Santiago, Chile, Central Bank of Chile, pp. 171–219.

Phillips, A. W. (1958), 'The relation between unemployment and the rate of change of money wages in the United Kingdom 1861–1957', *Economica*, NS 25(2), 283–99.

Razzak, W. A. (2002), 'Monetary policy and forecasting inflation with and without the output gap', *Reserve Bank of New Zealand,* Discussion Paper Series, March.

Reyes, J. (2003), 'Inflation targeting in emerging economies: exchange rate pressure', *mimeo*, July.

Sánchez, O., J. Seade and A. Werner (1999), 'Los Costos Asociados al Proceso Desinflacionario', *Banco de México*, Documento de investigación No. 9903.

Schaechter, A., M. R. Stone and M. Zelmer (2000), 'Adopting inflation targeting: practical issues for emerging market Countries', *IMF Occasional Paper*, 202, Washington, DC.

Shapiro, M. D. and M. W. Watson (1998), 'Sources of business cycle fluctuations', in O. J. Blanchard and S. Fischer (eds), *NBER Macroeconomics Annual*, MIT Press, Cambridge, MA.

7
External Debt Dynamics and Growth: A Neo-Keynesian Perspective

Edgardo Jovero

7.1 Introduction

Risk refers to the volatility of returns on investment. Global risk refers to the volatility on investment situated in a globalized economy. In macroeconomics, there exist two dominant schools of thought explaining the importance of volatility or short-term fluctuations in studying the behaviour of aggregate variables such as investment.

The neoclassical school views short-term fluctuations or volatility in investment behaviour as unimportant since the aggregate economy possesses what is termed 'structural stability' by which a unique and globally stable fixed-point equilibrium exists. This means that long-term growth is more important than short-term volatility.

The Keynesians, on the other hand, view short-term volatility as an important source of business cycle fluctuations that deserves to be studied on its own. Moreover, it becomes imperative to design optimal government policy interventions to dampen such volatile and cyclical behaviour.

In this chapter, an open-economy neo-Keynesian model is developed which highlights market power and price-setting behaviour as a source of indeterminacy and structural instability to explain the varying experiences on growth and external debt of different countries sharing the same fundamentals. Unlike the earlier studies on external debt and growth, this proposed new model will focus on the likely existence of indeterminate solutions and how this new highlight on the dynamic relationship between external debt and growth may be a more realistic theoretical explanation for the varying experiences of several countries. This should contribute to a better understanding of the global risk environment that international investment managers face.

7.2 The macroeconomics of growth and fluctuations: an introductory note

Until recently, in macroeconomics there existed a big gap between models emphasizing short-term fluctuations versus models focusing on long-term growth. Such differentiation in focus gave way to two paths in dynamic modelling in macroeconomics. One genre of models focusing on short-term fluctuations belonged to the Keynesian school emphasizing the sources of short-term fluctuations in an economy such as 'menu costs' and 'sluggish adjustments'. In this genre of works one might find Blanchard and Kiyotaki's 'quality-adjustment' model. Other types of studies include some of the more important OLG monetary models of the Cagan-type where monetary shocks such as that of Diamond and Samuelson produce endogenous fluctuations in the economy, and totally rejecting the super-neutrality of money (see Flaschel *et al.* (1997) and Rosser (2000) for a detailed discussion on this).

The other genre of macroeconomic models focuses on long-term growth and these models concentrate on neoclassical types including those of the Solow–Swan model as well as the 'modern growth models' of Paul Romer and Lucas. Here the emphasis is on long-term growth and convergence.

Later a new breed of macroeconomic modellers attempted to fuse these two approaches as in the pioneering works of Grandmont (1986), Medio (1987) and Benhabib and Nishimura (1987), which demonstrated that neoclassical growth models although being deterministic in nature are capable of producing 'endogenous fluctuations' without the need for exogenous shocks. The modern agenda in macroeconomic modelling thus emphasizes the fusion between long-term growth and short-term fluctuations.

The result of this fusion gave rise to models with 'deterministic chaotic behavior' or more commonly 'nonlinear models with endogenous fluctuations'. In the present study, there is an attempt to contribute to this recent trend by analyzing the behaviour of an open-economy two-sector growth model in the tradition of the neo-Keynesian non-market clearing emphasis. The main contribution of this chapter is that it has been able to prove the existence of indeterminacy by which a stable region is connected to an unstable region situated in a centre manifold in the state-space of the resulting dynamical system.

In explaining such a phenomenon, a two-good dependent open-economy endowed with endogenous growth, which engenders an indeterminate solution (in the form of short-term 'chaotic fluctuations' and long-term unpredictability) is developed. The dependent open-economy assumes that the economy is small, that is, it is subject to a given international interest rate which it cannot influence.

7.3 External debt dynamics and growth, a proposed neo-Keynesian model

Let us begin by assuming the existence of a Robinson Crusoe-type of closed economy where there are only two types of goods – a consumption good (C) and a capital good (K). The representative agent consumes C to derive a level of satisfaction or utility which he maximizes in an iso-elastic CRRA utility function to be formulated later. K is saved to be used in the next period using a production function of the form: $Y = AK$. Y is output, A is a fixed production coefficient determining the level of technology held constant through time.

To begin the analysis, we first assume a closed economy where the intertemporal budget constraint is binding in every period. This is expressed as: $Y = C + I$, where I is the change in the capital stock or real investment such that $I = \dot{K}$.

Investment, in the economic sense, refers to the change in the capital stock in real terms, and has to be formed from what is left over from consumption such that $Y - C = I = S$, for S = savings. The model is formulated in continuous time such that: $I = \dot{K}$.

Now, reformulate the intertemporal budget constraint to focus on the internationalization of the economy. Assume that international borrowing and lending is possible, such that $Y - C = S \neq I$. This means that savings is no longer equal to investment at any one time.

We have the following:

$$\dot{D} = rD + C + I\left(1 + \frac{I}{K}\right) - AK$$

This is the standard intertemporal budget constraint for an open-economy which is incorporated in a standard balance of payments (BOP) double-entry accounting: The capital account may be represented as: $\dot{D} - rD$, which shows all the receipts (both debit and credit entries) on financial assets. The current account may be represented as: $C + I - AK$, which includes all the entries on the flow of tangible goods or commodities. In standard double-entry BOP accounting (using the domestic absorption approach): the capital account = the current account.

It is to be noted that such a budget constraint applies only to the case where there is perfect competition in the international financial market, that is, where the price of debt equals its marginal cost ($r = p = MC$). In recent years however, the current trend in international finance has questioned this assumption of perfect competition. Rather a more realistic assumption is that of price-setting behaviour or monopolistic competition. The main evidence presented is the existence of a secondary market for debt issues of developing countries. Thus, $r \neq MC$, which means that the price of debt is no longer equal to its marginal cost, which in turn is equal to the international interest rate. Therefore, in the secondary market, debt-bonds can be sold at a discount up to the point where the true cost of the debt equals the international interest rate plus a mark-up margin for profit.

Given this imperfect competition situation, many authors in international trade and finance or in what is termed the new open-economy macroeconomics have reformulated the intertemporal budget constraint to highlight this price-setting behaviour of the suppliers of debt. One famous and well-studied (almost standard) formulation of this is by Turnovsky (1997), following models developed by Bardhan. In this formulation, a risk-premium parameter is added such that:

$$\dot{D} = rD + R\left(\frac{D}{K}\right) + C + I\left(1 + \frac{I}{K}\right) - AK$$

As interpreted by Turnovsky (1999), the term *R(D/K)* represents the elasticity of debt to the capital stock. Capital is viewed here as a collateral, and a high (*D/K*) ratio represent a high risk of default in the future repayment of the principal and the interest on debt. *R* is assumed constant, but its effect is influenced by *(D/K)*. We now formulate the model:

$$\text{Max } U = \int_{t=0}^{t=\infty}\left(\frac{C^{1-\sigma}}{1-\sigma}\right)e^{-\rho t}dt \tag{7.1}$$

$$\text{s.t. } \dot{D} = rD + R\left(\frac{D}{K}\right) + C + I\left(1 + \frac{I}{K}\right) - AK \tag{7.2}$$

$$\dot{K} = I \tag{7.3}$$

with initial values at $K(0) = K_0$; $D(0) = D_0$.

Applying optimal control theory, formulate the current-value Hamiltonian:

$$H_c = \left(\frac{C^{1-\sigma}}{1-\sigma}\right) + \lambda\left[rD + R\left(\frac{D}{K}\right) + C + I\left(1 + \frac{I}{K}\right) - AK\right] + q(I) \tag{7.4}$$

The Pontryagin maximum conditions are:

$$\frac{\partial H_c}{\partial C} = 0 = C^{-\sigma} + \lambda \tag{7.5}$$

or this is simplified as: $C^{-\sigma} = -\lambda$. Taking logs: $-\sigma \log C = -\log \lambda$; and time derivatives: $-\sigma(\dot{C}/C) = -(\dot{\lambda}/\lambda)$. Or simplifying: $(\dot{C}/C) = (1/\sigma)(\dot{\lambda}/\lambda)$; for $\sigma \neq 0$.

The second condition requires that

$$\frac{\partial H_c}{\partial D} = -\dot{\lambda} + \rho\lambda = \lambda\left(r + R\left(\frac{D}{K}\right)\right) \tag{7.6}$$

This can be simplified as:

$$\frac{-\dot{\lambda}}{\lambda} + \rho = r + \frac{R}{K} \tag{7.7}$$

$$\frac{\dot{\lambda}}{\lambda} = -r - \left(\frac{R}{K}\right) + \rho \tag{7.8}$$

Assuming strict consumption smoothing (which is logical since the model is situated in an open-economy environment, where access to international borrowing and lending results in strict consumption smoothing) such that ($r = \rho$), then equation 7.8 may be rewritten as:

$$\frac{\dot{\lambda}}{\lambda} = -\frac{R}{K} \tag{7.9}$$

This can combine with Equation 7.6 such that:

$$\frac{\dot{C}}{C} = \left(\frac{1}{\sigma}\right)\left(-\frac{R}{K}\right) \tag{7.10}$$

or this can be simplified as:

$$\frac{\dot{C}}{C} = -\frac{R}{\sigma K} \tag{7.11}$$

In equilibrium, ($\dot{\lambda}/\lambda$) is equal to zero so that the first of the transversality conditions (to be specified later) has to be fulfilled. Therefore, needless to say, ($\dot{C}/C$) must necessarily be equal to zero which is an equilibrium condition.

Then to continue with the maximum first-order conditions:

$$\frac{\partial H_c}{\partial K} = -\dot{q} + \rho q = \frac{-\lambda RD}{K^2} + \frac{-\lambda I^2}{K^2} - \lambda A \tag{7.12}$$

Here q is taken to be the adjustment cost of capital K, so that total investment increases by incurring a higher adjustment cost, as explained in Blachard and Fischer (1989).

Simplifying,

$$\frac{\dot{q}}{q} = \left(\frac{\lambda}{q}\right)\left(\frac{R}{K}\right)\left(\frac{D}{K}\right) + \left(\frac{\lambda}{q}\right)\left(\frac{\dot{K}}{K}\right)^2 + \left(\frac{\lambda}{q}\right)A + r$$

In equilibrium $(\dot{q}/q)$ should be equal to zero to fulfill the famous transversality condition. As such, in equilibrium, investment is held constant so that a constant stock of capital is kept for all times. Another condition is that in equilibrium, investment is zero such that a constant level of capital stock (K) is maintained. Therefore supply of K needs to be maintained at a constant level in every period so that the production of the consumption good C continues. From this equation a simplified accumulation equation for the optimal capital stock (or the optimal investment decision) is defined as:

$$\frac{\dot{K}}{K} = \left[-\left(\frac{R}{K}\right)\left(\frac{D}{K}\right) - A - r\left(\frac{q}{\lambda}\right)\right]^{\frac{1}{2}} = 0 \tag{7.13}$$

The dynamical system is rewritten as follows:

$$\frac{\dot{C}}{C} = \frac{-R}{\sigma K} = 0 \tag{7.14}$$

$$\frac{\dot{K}}{K} = \left[-\left(\frac{R}{K}\right)\left(\frac{D}{K}\right) - A - r\left(\frac{q}{\lambda}\right)\right]^{\frac{1}{2}} = 0 \tag{7.15}$$

$$\frac{\dot{D}}{D} = r + \left(\frac{R}{K}\right) + \left(\frac{C}{D}\right) - A\left(\frac{K}{D}\right) = 0 \tag{7.16}$$

$$\frac{\dot{\lambda}}{\lambda} = -\frac{R}{K} = 0 \tag{7.17}$$

$$\frac{\dot{q}}{q} = \left(\frac{\lambda}{q}\right)\left(\frac{R}{K}\right)\left(\frac{D}{K}\right) + \left(\frac{\lambda}{q}\right)A + r = 0 \tag{7.18}$$

The transversality conditions are:

$$\lim_{t \to \infty} \mathrm{e}^{-\rho t}\lambda(t)D(t) = 0$$

$$\lim_{t \to \infty} \mathrm{e}^{-\rho t}q(t)K(t) = 0$$

The above dynamical system shows an indeterminate path for the accumulation of K. This is the indeterminacy situation where the transversality conditions are insufficient to guarantee the uniqueness nor the existence of an equilibrium balance growth path for both the state and control variables.

For instance in analyzing Equation 7.17, one can see that this requires R to be equal to 0, and K can take on any value. Such a situation is common in so-called 'endogenous growth models'. There are two ways by which macroeconomists deal with this problem. One popular method is that proposed by Caballè and Santos (1993) which has been further developed by Ortiguiera and Santos (1994). This method imposes a common growth rate on the dynamical system to solve for a balanced growth path (BSP) solution. This is done by adding a common growth rate to all of the state and control variables, while allowing the dynamic multipliers to share a different common growth rate.

The other method is proposed by Mulligan and Sala-i-Martin (1991, 1993) who developed the so-called 'time-elimination method' which will also be used in this chapter. In solving the system, a change of variable is undertaken such that:

$$s(t) = \frac{C(t)}{D(t)}$$

$$d(t) = \frac{D(t)}{K(t)}$$

$$w(t) = \frac{\lambda(t)}{q(t)}$$

$$Q = \frac{R}{K}$$

Q is assumed constant.

Taking logs and time derivatives:

$$\frac{\dot{s}}{s} = \frac{\dot{C}}{C} - \frac{\dot{D}}{D}$$

$$\frac{\dot{d}}{d} = \frac{\dot{D}}{D} - \frac{\dot{K}}{K}$$

$$\frac{\dot{w}}{w} = \frac{\dot{\lambda}}{\lambda} - \frac{\dot{q}}{q}$$

The new dynamical system is now expressed as:

$$\frac{\dot{s}}{s} = \left(-\frac{Q}{\sigma}\right) - r - Q - s - \left(\frac{A}{d}\right) = 0 \qquad (7.19)$$

$$\frac{\dot{d}}{d} = r + Q + s - \left(\frac{A}{d}\right) - \left(-Qd - A - \frac{r}{w}\right)^{\frac{1}{2}} = 0 \qquad (7.20)$$

$$\frac{\dot{w}}{w} = -Q - wQd - wA - r = 0 \qquad (7.21)$$

with the new state variables s, d and w not equated to 0.

Applying the Hartman–Grobman theorem on linearization, the result obtained is as follows:

$$\begin{bmatrix} \dot{s} \\ \dot{d} \\ \dot{w} \end{bmatrix} = A \begin{bmatrix} s \\ d \\ w \end{bmatrix} + \begin{bmatrix} s - s^* \\ d - d^* \\ w - w^* \end{bmatrix} \quad \text{for } s^*, d^*, w^* \text{ as equilibrium values}$$

A is the Jacobian of first derivatives such that the entries $a_{ij} = \partial F_i / \partial x_j$, for i = 1st, 2nd, 3rd equation and $j = s,w,d$. In this case, the indeterminacy arises when one of the eigenvalues of A is equal to 0 completely or if the real part of a complex root is zero. This means that the dynamical system is non-hyperbolic in the language of dynamics, and linearization fails.

This is easily proven by solving for the zeroes of the associated characteristic polynomial of the canonical Jacobian matrix. A simple examination of the Jacobian shows this:

$$A = \begin{bmatrix} \frac{\partial F_1}{\partial s} & \frac{\partial F_2}{\partial d} & \frac{\partial F_3}{\partial w} \\ \frac{\partial F_2}{\partial s} & \frac{\partial F_2}{\partial d} & \frac{\partial F_2}{\partial w} \\ \frac{\partial F_3}{\partial s} & \frac{\partial F_3}{\partial d} & \frac{\partial F_3}{\partial w} \end{bmatrix} = \begin{bmatrix} a_{11} & a_{12} & a_{13} \\ a_{21} & a_{22} & a_{23} \\ a_{13} & a_{32} & a_{33} \end{bmatrix}$$

The entries of the Jacobian matrix A are defined as follows:

$$a_{11} = \left(-\frac{Q}{\sigma}\right) - r - Q - 2s - \left(\frac{A}{d}\right)$$

$$a_{12} = \frac{As}{d^2}$$

$$a_{13} = 0$$

$$a_{21} = d$$

$$a_{22} = r + Q + s$$

$$+ \left[\left(\frac{dQ}{2} \right) \left(-Qd - A - \frac{r}{w} \right)^{-\frac{1}{2}} + \left(-Qd - A - \frac{r}{w} \right)^{\frac{1}{2}} \right]$$

$$a_{23} = \left[\left(\frac{dr}{2w^2} \right) \left(-Qd - A - \frac{r}{w} \right)^{-\frac{1}{2}} \right]$$

$$a_{31} = 0$$
$$a_{32} = -w^2 Q$$
$$a_{33} = -Q - 2wQd - 2wA - r$$

Setting $x_i = A\exp(\lambda t)$; for λ = the associated eigenvalues of the dynamical system, then for det $|A - I\lambda| = 0$; the characteristic polynomial is defined as follows:

$$p(\lambda) = \det|A - I\lambda| = \det \begin{vmatrix} a_{11} - \lambda & a_{12} & a_{13} \\ a_{21} & a_{22} - \lambda & a_{23} \\ a_{31} & a_{32} & a_{33} - \lambda \end{vmatrix} = 0$$

$$\begin{aligned} p(\lambda) = & -\lambda^3 + (a_{11} + a_{22} + a_{33})\lambda^2 \\ & - [(a_{11}a_{22} - a_{12}a_{21}) + (a_{11}a_{33} - a_{13}a_{31}) \\ & + (a_{22}a_{33} - a_{23}a_{32})]\lambda \\ & + (a_{11}a_{22}a_{33} + a_{12}a_{23}a_{31} + a_{13}a_{21}a_{32} \\ & - a_{13}a_{22}a_{31} - a_{11}a_{23}a_{32} - a_{12}a_{21}a_{33}) \\ = & \ 0 \end{aligned}$$

$$p(\lambda) = -\lambda^3 + T\lambda - M\lambda + D = 0$$

This last equation can also be rewritten as

$$p(\lambda) = \lambda^3 - T\lambda^2 + M\lambda - D = 0.$$

This is further defined for the following variables:

$$T = \text{trace of } A = \sum a_{ii}$$

$$M = \begin{vmatrix} a_{11} & a_{12} \\ a_{21} & a_{22} \end{vmatrix} + \begin{vmatrix} a_{11} & a_{13} \\ a_{31} & a_{33} \end{vmatrix} + \begin{vmatrix} a_{22} & a_{23} \\ a_{32} & a_{33} \end{vmatrix}$$
$$= \text{sum of the diagonal minors of } A$$
$$D = \det |A|$$

An eigenvector associated with the eigenvalue λ_i is the vector (v_1,v_2,v_3) satisfying the equality $\lambda_i v_i = A\lambda_i$. An eigenvector may be complex if λ_i is complex. In this case, there is a complex conjugate pair of eigenvalues and eigenvectors in this eigensystem. Note also that the following relationships hold:

$$\lambda_1 + \lambda_2 + \lambda_3 = T$$
$$\lambda_1\lambda_2 + \lambda_1\lambda_3 + \lambda_2\lambda_3 = M$$
$$\lambda_1\lambda_2\lambda_3 = D$$

For a_{ij} all real, then D, T and M are either all real, or it may be that only one eigenvalue is real and the other two are a pair of complex conjugate eigenvalues (see Jackson, 1998; Perko, 2000; Puu, 2003).

From here, one can apply standard bifurcation theory by hypothesizing that the stability condition of the eigensystem (whether only negative real roots exist as a solution) is a function of a bifurcation parameter – in this model of Q (the market-power parameter which measures the ability of the debt supplier to influence the interest cost of debt, that is, the price-setting power of the debt-supplier).

The next step in analyzing the behaviour (i.e. its limiting behaviour as time approaches infinity) is to show structural stability. This entails testing whether the system finally settles down to a unique and globally stable steady state equilibrium as time goes to infinity, irrespective of any small perturbation in any of the system's parameters. Or alternatively, one can also test whether the dynamical system is capable of demonstrating more complex behaviour such as the presence of strange attractors or of Hopf bifurcation. Complex dynamics arise when the system's state-space geometry is completely changed for any minute perturbation in a bifurcation parameter. This characterizes 'structural instability' in the state-space solution of the dynamical system.

One way of testing this is to locate the roots of the associated characteristic polynomial relatively with respect to the imaginary axis.

If one root lies in the imaginary axis, then pure complex roots in conjugates are at work. This is a necessary but not sufficient condition for nonlinear complex dynamical behaviour that allows a Hopf bifurcation to arise. The most convenient way of root-location is by applying Routh–Hurwitz (R–H) theorem.[1]

Applying the theorem for the cubic characteristic polynomial with $n = 3$, the dynamical system above can be formulated in terms of the R–H array as follows:

$$\begin{array}{c|cc} \lambda^3 & a_0 & a_2 \\ \lambda^2 & a_1 & a_3 \\ \lambda^1 & (a_1 a_2 - a_0 a_3)/a_1 & 0 \\ \lambda^0 & a_3 & \end{array} = \begin{array}{|cc} 1 & M \\ -T & -D \\ T + (D/M) & 0 \\ -D & \end{array}$$

The stability condition for a cubic characteristic polynomial as we have is stated as follows: $a > 0$; $(a_1 a_2 - a_0 a_3) > 0$; $a_3 > 0$ which is the same as saying that $T < 0$; $D < 0$; $TM <$ D. This would ensure that the entries in the dominant column in the R–H array are all positive. This means that all the roots are in the left-hand plane of the imaginary axis (i.e. the stable manifold) and the dynamical system possesses structural stability in the global sense.

Combining the R–H theorem with the rule of signs of Descartes for polynomials,[2] it can be shown that for a cubic characteristic polynomial, there are only two cases to consider: either all the roots are real (for $\lambda_i \subset R$) including zero and multiplicities, or only one is real and there exists a pair of complex conjugates ($\lambda_{i=1,2} \subset C$). Thus the solution set for the dynamical system can be expressed as either one of the two cases:

$$\begin{bmatrix} \lambda_1 & 0 & 0 \\ 0 & \lambda_2 & 0 \\ 0 & 0 & \lambda_3 \end{bmatrix} \quad \begin{bmatrix} \lambda_1 & 0 & 0 \\ 0 & \alpha & \beta \\ 0 & -\beta & \alpha \end{bmatrix}$$

Liu (1994), Seydel (1994), Wiggins (2004) as well as Guckenheimer *et al.* (1997) provide ample discussions on the requirements for case 2 to arise, whereby a bifurcation plane exists and for which a possible Hopf bifurcation is embedded. In the case of a cubic characteristic polynomial ($n = 3$), the sufficient and necessary conditions for a Hopf bifurcation to arise are: $(\partial p(\lambda;\, Q))/\partial Q \neq 0$, and $T < 0$, $D < 0$ and $TM = D$.

The last requirement that $TM = D$ is an extension of the R–H theorem. The theorem indicates that for an odd-numbered row in the

R–H array containing all zeroes, there is then a necessary but not sufficient condition for pure complex roots to exist. This means that the roots are located exactly in the imaginary axis itself with the real part being zero. In addition, the signs of the column entries preceding and succeeding this zero entry must be the same.

When these conditions are met, there exists a non-hyperbolic root which means that either $\det|A| = 0$ or a pair of pure complex roots exist, and the linearization theorem (Hartman–Grobman) fails. This goes to show that the system is indeterminate. For such non-hyperbolic (or indeterminate) systems, a centre manifold exists,[3] which means one of the roots contains either zero or pure complex numbers. For such non-linear dynamical systems, Sotomayor's theorem is applied such that:

$$\begin{bmatrix} \dot{s} \\ \dot{d} \\ \dot{w} \end{bmatrix} = A \begin{bmatrix} s \\ d \\ w \end{bmatrix} + B_Q \begin{bmatrix} s \\ d \\ w \end{bmatrix} + \begin{bmatrix} s - s^* \\ d - d^* \\ w - w^* \end{bmatrix}$$

for $B_Q = \partial^2 F_i / \partial x_j \partial Q$, evaluated at the equilibrium values of s, d and w.

Sotomayor's theorem specifies the existence of a bifurcation type of generic behaviour given that for an eigenvector v not equal to 0, which is associated with one of the simple 0 or pure complex conjugate roots as eigenvalues of A, the following holds: $vB_Q \neq 0$.

For the dynamic system above this is expressed as:

$$\begin{bmatrix} v_1 \\ v_2 \\ v_3 \end{bmatrix} \begin{bmatrix} \left(-\frac{1}{\sigma}\right) - 1 & 0 & 0 \\ 0 & 1 + \left[\left(\frac{Q}{4}\right)\left(-Qd - A - \frac{r}{w}\right)^{-\frac{3}{2}} + \left(\frac{d}{2}\right)\left(-Qd - A - \frac{r}{w}\right)^{-\frac{1}{2}}\right] & \left(\frac{r}{4w^2}\right)\left(-Qd - A - \frac{r}{w}\right)^{-\frac{3}{2}} \\ 0 & -w^2 & -2wd \end{bmatrix} \neq O_3$$

O_3 is the 3×3 null matrix. Sotomayor's theorem was developed to investigate the generic behaviour of non-hyperbolic 2×2 systems, and has been extended to higher dimensions by Smale and V. Arnold, the Russian dynamicist. Furthermore, the role of Q as a bifurcation parameter can be expressed as follows:

$$p(\lambda;Q) = \lambda^3 - T\lambda^2 + M\lambda - D = 0 \tag{7.22}$$

$$\frac{\partial p(\lambda;Q)}{\partial Q} = \left(\frac{\partial p(\lambda;Q)}{\partial T}\right)\left(\frac{\partial T}{\partial Q}\right) + \left(\frac{\partial p(\lambda;Q)}{\partial M}\right)\left(\frac{\partial M}{\partial Q}\right) + \left(\frac{\partial p(\lambda;Q)}{\partial D}\right)\left(\frac{\partial D}{\partial Q}\right) \neq 0 \tag{7.23}$$

$$\frac{\partial p(\lambda;Q)}{\partial Q} = (-2\lambda)T'(Q) + M'(Q) - D'(Q) \neq 0 \tag{7.24}$$

Therefore the bifurcation boundary can be defined in terms of the following:

$$\lambda = \frac{M'(Q) - D'(Q)}{2T'(Q)} = 0.$$

This can be simulated to illustrate geometrically the role of Q as a bifurcation parameter using the following constant values ($A = 1$, $r = 0.2$, $\sigma = 0.15$ and equilibrium values of $d = 1$, $s = 1$, and $w = 0.01$). The geometrical illustration of Q as a bifurcation parameter may be shown by the following equation:

$$\lambda = \frac{k_1Q^2 + k_2Q + k_3}{2k_4}$$

Figures 7.1(a)–(c) that follow provide various illustrations of the possible eigenspace formed and of the effect of Q on the eigenvalues.

Figure 7.1(a) shows how the different values of the determinant, the trace and the M (the sum of the principal minors) of the Jacobian can be affected by Q (the parameter describing the markup power of the debt supplier). One can also see how the stability region of the eigenspace is formed for negative values of the determinant and the trace.

In Figure 7.1(b), the necessary (but not sufficient) condition that the determinant be equal to the sum of the trace (T) and M is illustrated. As can be seen, a substantial portion of the eigenspace of solutions, which describes the possible behaviour of the nonlinear dynamic model in Equations 7.19 to 7.21, contains a bifurcation region where $D = TM$. This is also where a pair of pure complex roots exists as an eigensolution set . The dynamic behaviour in this region is characterized by the Hopf bifurcation, where strange attractors reign. This describes global instability and the impossibility of long-term prediction.[4]

In Figure 7.1(c), one can see how varying values in Q significantly affect the stability – instability characteristic of the non-linear dynamical system as summarized by Equations 7.19–7.21. Figure 7.1(c) also shows that for larger and larger values of Q, the behaviour of the

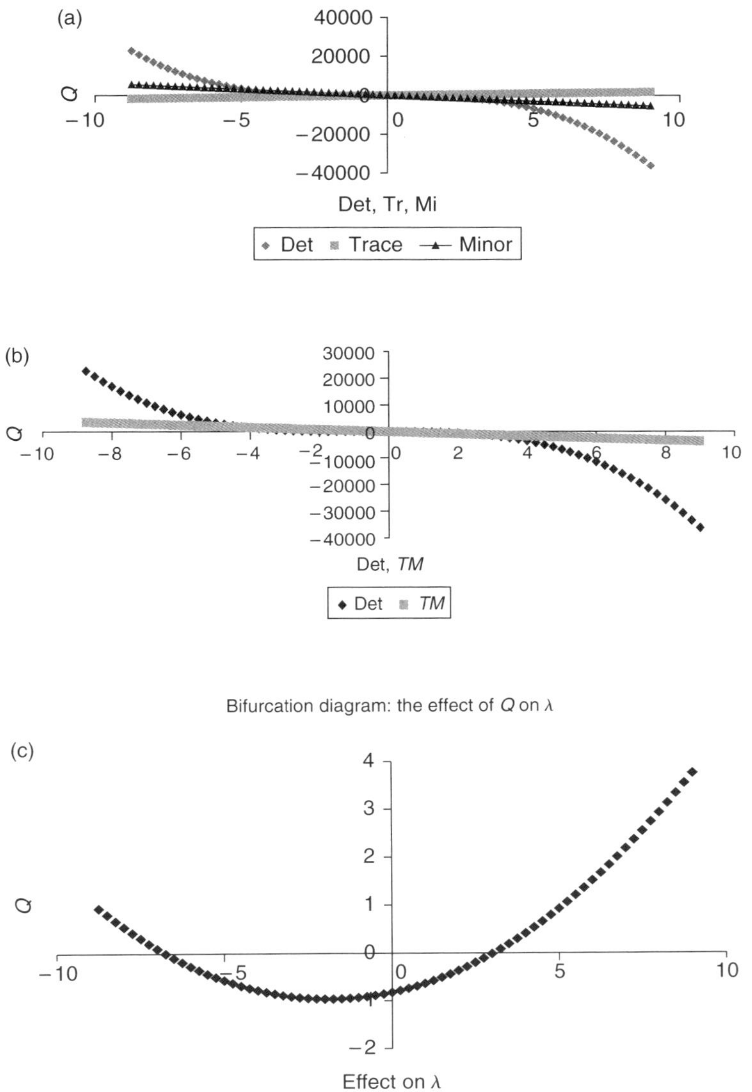

Figure 7.1 (a) The state-space boundaries of the dynamical model; (b) Region of the state-space where Det = *TM*; (c) The bifurcation boundary of the state-space

dynamical system shifts from stability to instability. This is a sign of structural instability, whereby minute changes in a bifurcation parameter (in this case of *Q*) results in significant changes in the geometry of dynamical system's state space.

The fact that *Q* acts as a bifurcation parameter, together with conditions 7.22–7.24 form both the sufficient and necessary conditions for the Hopf bifurcation phenomenon to exit in the eigensolution space of the nonlinear dynamical system.[5] A Hopf bifurcation forms when the dynamical system is inherently capable of what is known as 'self-excitation'. This means that the dynamical system is capable of producing endogenous erratic fluctuations, as a stable attractive eigenvalue an suddenly turn unstable (repelling), without any significant stimulus from an external source.

The dynamics can be also geometrically studied through the simulation of the dynamical system for different values of *Q*. This was done in Matlab using the ode23s solver for stiff nonlinear dynamical sytems of differential equations. The simulation was carried out using values of 1 for *A* (the technological coefficient), 0.15 for sigma (the aggregate demand parameter representing the inverse of the intertemporal rate of substitution for present versus future consumption or the level of impatience for present consumption of the representative agent), and 0.2 for *r* (the exogenously given international rate of interest). Figures 7.1(a)–(e) show the behaviour of the system for different values of *Q* at 0.1, 0.5, 1.0, 5.0 and 10.

Comparing Figures 7.2(a)–(e), one can see that a change in *Q* does not drastically alter the behaviour of s which is the consumption-to-debt ratio and is drawn as a blue line. It is downward sloping through time because debt increases while the consumption is being kept constant.

On the other hand, one can see that for the same set of figures, the debt-to-capital ratio (d), drawn as a green line, is changing its behaviour significantly through time as *Q* is changed from 0.1 to 10.0. This shows that the behaviour of the capital stock fluctuates significantly through time as *Q* is changed. In the dynamical literature, this is referred to as a bifurcation.[6]

In comparing Figures 7.3(a)–(e), it is seen that bifurcation occurs when the two ratios are drawn in one graph. In Figure 7.3(a), a perceptible homoclinic loop arises. This is characteristic of a bifurcation (see Guckenheimer and Holmes, 1995; Jackson, 1999) phenomenon where a single loop is discernible. Inside the loop, an attracting set

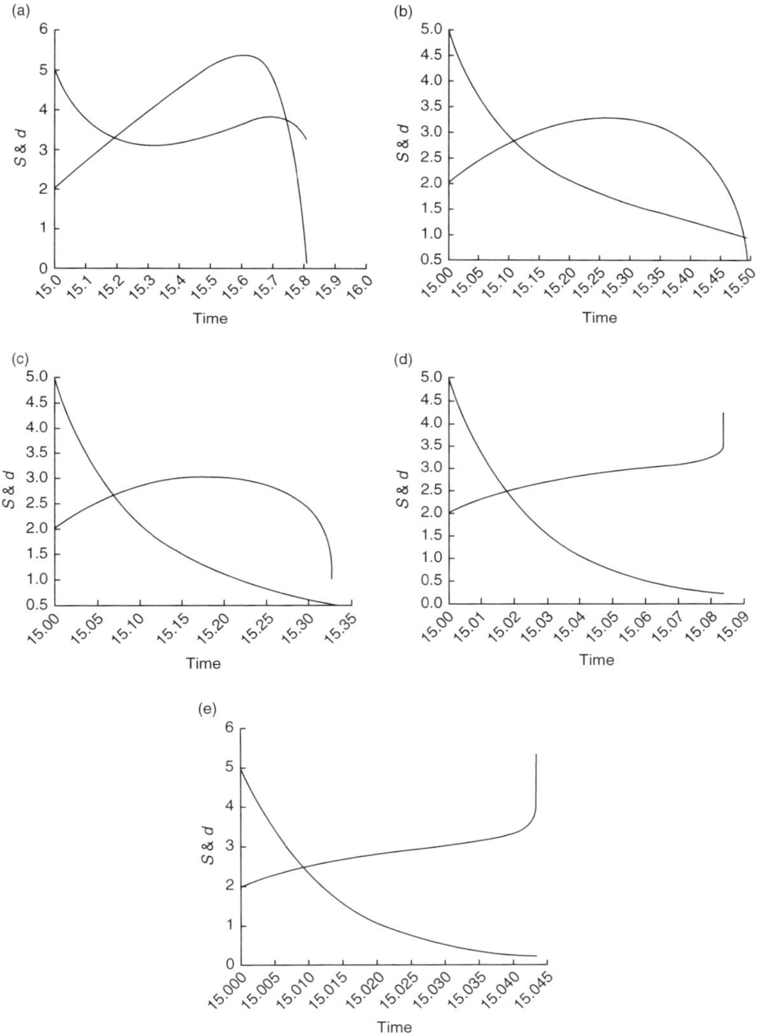

Figure 7.2 (a) Estimation 23 Nov. 2003, for $A = 1$ and $Q = 0.1$; (b) Estimation 23 Nov. 2003, for $A = 1$ and $Q = 0.5$; (c) Estimation 23 Nov. 2003, for $A = 1$ and $Q = 1$; (d) Estimation 23 Nov. 2003, for $A = 1$ and $Q = 5$; (e) Estimation 23 Nov. 2003, for $A = 1$ and $Q = 10$

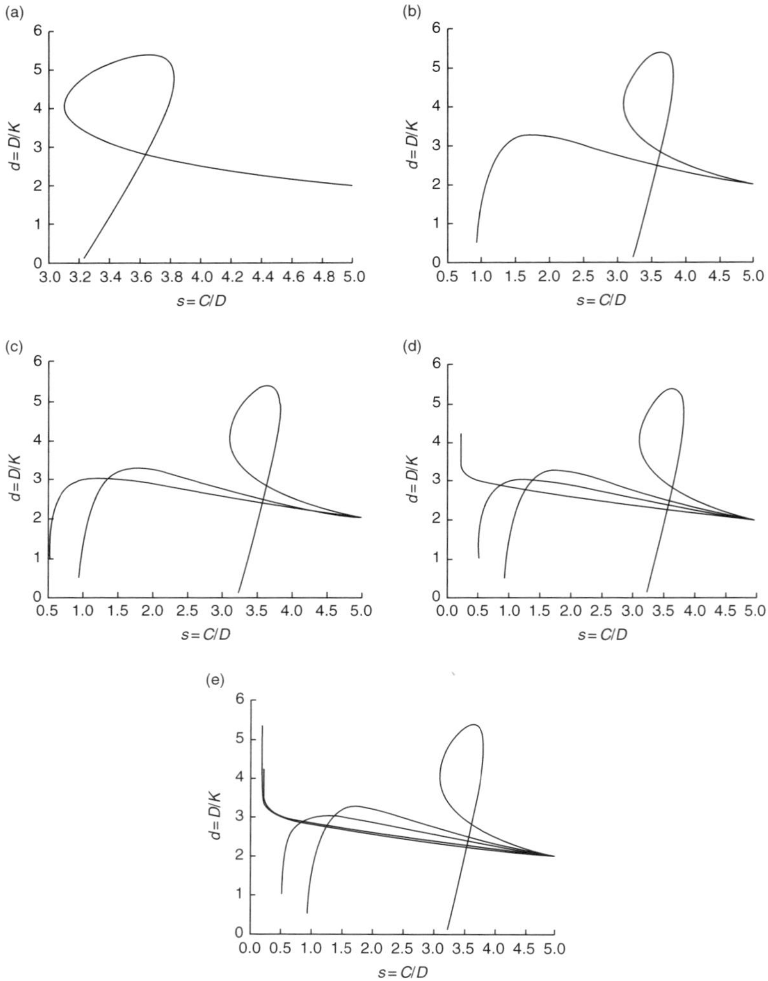

Figure 7.3 (a) s–d plot for $Q = 0.1$; (b) s–d plot for $Q = 0.5$; (c) s–d plot for $Q = 1$; (d) s–d plot for $Q = 5$; (e) s–d plot for $Q = 10$

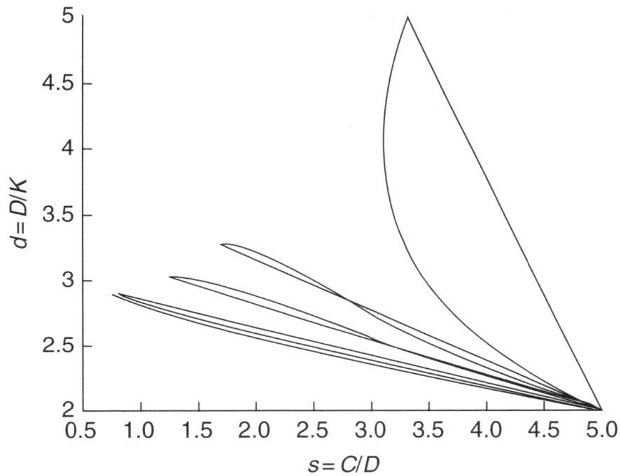

Figure 7.4 *s–d* plot for different values of $Q = 0.1, 0.5, 1, 5$ and 10

exists which can represent a low-development or low-growth trap. Any trajectory which begins inside the loop will be trapped forever inside this loop. The loop itself represents an escape route from this attracting set. An economy with initial conditions close to but not inside the loop will not enter the trapping region, but escape towards higher levels of growth.

It is important to state that this type of dynamic analysis for nonlinear models is allowed only for local points of equilibrium and not in a global sense. The global behaviour of nonlinear systems (of order $n \geq 3$) is still not completely known. However, in the model discussed in the chapter, structural instability exists in the global sense with the formation of a Hopf bifurcation phenomenon. Specifically, the Hopf bifurcation is a consequence of the destruction of the homoclinic loop (as shown in Figure 7.3(a)) which represents global stability in the form of regular limit cycles.

With regard to the model's importance in the analysis of external debt and growth issues, one should take note that there is no simple linear relationship. Rather a complex nonlinear model is proposed to be more suitable. Furthermore, variables which form part of the fundamentals of an economy (such as technology and taste, e.g., A and σ in the model above) are not necessary to provoke fluctuations in investment and debt behaviour, contrary to the prediction of the neoclassical view on real business cycles.

Rather a non-fundamental variable (Q, which represents market power in the international finance market) is deemed more likely to provoke changes in the way an economy would experience the effect of external debt on growth.

7.4 Summarizing the results

The main topic of this chapter is to rebuke the neoclassical emphasis on global uniqueness and saddle-path stability in growth models where the economic agent is endowed with rational expectations and perfect foresight. In terms of modern dynamic analysis, neoclassical growth models exhibit 'structural stability' which does not allow for the existence of a centre manifold, where short-term fluctuations can have permanent and structural effects on the global behaviour of the aggregate economy.

The Lyapunov–Poincaré[7] definition of structural stability places strong emphasis on the fact that a slight change in a control or bifurcation parameter would not in any way modify the geometry of the state-space of a dynamical system. This property is present in the global saddle-path stability of the neoclassical growth model. Within the neoclassical tradition, the strong emphasis on global and structural stability is shown to be consistent with rational expectations and perfect foresight which are imposed on the economic agent.

On the other hand, such global stability is not present in Keynesian models in general. This is consistent with Keynes's view that there exists *fundamental uncertainty* (see chapter 12 of the General Theory) in the aggregate economy (particularly in the international financial markets), by which policy (e.g. fiscal or monetary) can have a stabilizing role to play. This view is the basis for the neo-Keynesian dynamical model proposed in this chapter to explain the dynamic non-linear relationship between external debt and growth in an imperfect competitive environment where the debt supplier is endowed with market power.

This market power feature allows the debt supplier to charge a higher price on external debt received by different countries. It is seen that most often market power (i.e. the ability of debt suppliers to markup the price of external debt) is shown to be an important source of structural instability in the aggregate open-economy. It was stated earlier, that this structural instability can take the form of a Hopf bifurcation, the likelihood of which increases as the markup power (embodied in a variable called Q) increases. Some evidence is presented as to the likelihood of a Hopf bifurcation occurring, using the qualitative geometric theory of nonlinear dynamical systems. With Hopf bifurcation occurring, the neoclassical view of the economic agent endowed with rational expectations and perfect foresight is rejected. Instead, the Keynesian view that structural instability rules and therefore the need arises for policy to alleviate this instability in the form of dampened fluctuations is presented as an alternative view for macroeconomic theorizing.

Notes

The author wishes to thank the participants at the International Conference on Emerging Markets and Global Risk, especially Dr Sima Motamen-Samadian for her excellent organization efforts.

1. Standard references on Routh–Hurwitz are Gantmacher (1959) which contains a complete discussion of the proofs of R–H, as well as Barnett (1990) and Jackson (1999). A more comprehensive treatment is also found in Apostol (1997).
2. Consult any standard elementary algebra textbook on this, although Apostol (1997) as well as Gantmacher (1959) provide ample review of the topic.
3. A centre manifold allows for the existence of limit cycles as proposed by the Poincaré–Bendixson theorem. See Guckenheimer and Holmes (1999) as well as Perko (2000) and Jackson (1999) for details.
4. An excellent discussion of the Hopf bifurcation phenomenon is presented in Seydel (1994), Guckenheimer and Holmes (1997), Taylor (1999) and Puu (2003).
5. Liu (1997) and Guckenheimer *et al.* (1999) provide detailed theoretical discussions and proofs on this.
6. Technically, there is a very small difference in the use of 'catastrophe theory' which was originally formulated by René Thom and 'bifurcation theory' as formulated formally by Poincaré and Lyapunov. Strictly speaking, Thom's 'catastrophe theory' was developed using gradient systems, while 'bifurcation theory' is more general and encompasses 'catastrophe theory'. In recent years, writers have used the two terms interchangeably except to explicitly refer to Thom's theory (see Puu, 2003, on this).
7. See Guckenheimer and Holmes (1998), Jackson (1999) for a more technical discussion on the theorem and Tu (1999) and Puu (2003) for economic applications.

References

Apostol, T. (1997), *Linear Algebra, a First Course with Applications to Differential Equations*, John Wiley and Sons, Inc.

Barnett, S. (1990), *Matrices, Methods and Applications*, Oxford University Press, Oxford.

Benhabib, J. and K. Nishimura (1979), 'The Hopf bifurcation and the existence and stability of closed orbits in multisector models of optimal economic growth', *Journal of Economic Theory* 21, 421–44.

Benhabib, J. and K. Nishimura (1981), 'Stability of equilibrium and dynamic models of capital theory', *International Economic Review* 22, 275–93.

Blanchard, O. and S. Fisher. 1989. *Lectures in Macroeconomics*, MIT Press, Cambridge, MA.

Caballé, Jordi and Manuel Santos (1993), 'On endogenous growth with physical and human capital', *Journal of Political Economy* 101, 1042–68.

Flaschel, P., R. Frank and W. Semmler (1997), *Dynamic Macroeconomics, Instability, Fluctuations and Growth in Monetary Economics*, MIT Press, Cambridge, MA.

Gantmacher, F. R. (1959), *Applications of the Theory of Matrices*, Interscience Publishers, Inc., New York.

Grandmont, J. M. (1988), *Nonlinear Economic Dynamics*, Academic Press, New York.

Grandmont, J. M. (1990), *Economic Dynamics with Learning: Some Instability Examples*, CEPREMAP, Paris.

Guckenheimer, J. M. Myers and B. Sturmfels (1997), 'Computing Hopf bifurcations', *SIAM Journal of Numerical Analysis* 34, 1–21.

Guckenheimer, J. and P. Holmes, (1983), *Oscillations, Dynamical Systems and Bifurcation of Vector Fields*, Springer-Verlag, New York.

Jackson, E. A. (1990), *Perspectives of Nonlinear Dynamics*, Vols 1 & 2, Cambridge University Press, Cambridge, UK.

Liu, W.M. (1994), 'Criterion of Hopf bifurcation without using eigenvalues', *Journal of Mathematical Analysis and Applications* 182, 250–56.

Medio, A. (1991), 'Continuous-time models of chaos in economics', *Journal of Economic Behavior and Organization*, 16, 133–51.

Mulligan, C. and X. Sala-i-Martin (1991), A note on the time-elimination method for solving recursive economic models. Techical Working Paper No. 116, National Bureau of Economic Research, Massachusetts.

Mulligan, C. and X. Sala-i-Martin (1993), 'Transitional dynamics in two-sector models of endogenous growth', *Quarterly Journal of Economics* Aug, 1992, 739–773.

Ortigueira, S. and M. Santos (1994), On convergence in endogenous growth models. Working Paper WP94–54, Universidad Carlos III, Madrid.

Perko, L. (2000), *Differential Equations and Dynamical Systems*, Springer-Verlag, New York.

Puu, T. (2003), *Attractors, Bifurcations, and Chaos*, Springer, Berlin.

Rosser, Jr. J. B. (2000), *From Catastrophe to Chaos: A General Theory of Economic Discontinuities*, 2nd edn, Kluwer Academic Publishers, Boston.

Seydel, R. (1994), *Practical Bifurcation and Stability Analysis from Equilibrium to Chaos, Interdisciplinary Mathematics*, Vol. 5, 2nd edn, Springer-Verlag, New York.

Tu, P. (1994), *Dynamical Systems*, Springer-Verlag, Berlin.

Turnovsky, S. (1995), *Methods of Macroeconomic Dynamics*, MIT Press, Cambridge, MA.

Index